Branding Your Character

Living A Dynamic Life

Ken Owens

Praise for *Branding Your Character*

"*Branding Your Character* is a book I will refer to often. It is filled with research, inspiration, and practical tips that will support anyone wanting to establish and nurture their personal brand. Ken Owens is imminently qualified in this subject. I know him as someone who walks his talk! His persistence, integrity and passion for helping others are inspirational."
Gail Hurt, Career and Life Mentor
www.LivingAuthentically.com

"I've read MANY 'self-help' and psych books without any real 'interest' - this one not only held my attention but actually helped me too. This book made me recognize the need to develop my own 'personal brand'."
Mary Millard, Author

"*Branding Your Character* has convinced me that by following the principles therein the reader will create not only a strong professional brand, but will also develop the personal ability to have a positive impact upon society."
John Kirvan, Best-Selling Author: *30 Days With A Great Spiritual Teacher* series

Family Values / Parenting / Self Growth / Spirituality

Branding Your Character
Living A Fulfilled Life
by Ken Owens
www.BrandingYourCharacter.com

© 2012
Ken Owens
Las Vegas, NV USA
Email: ken@thekenowens.com
www.TheKenOwens.com

Cover design by: Elle Phillips
Ken's headshot by: Chuck Rounds

Personal Dynamics Publishing
www.PersonalDynamicsPublishing.com

ISBN: 978-0-615-55196-8

For those who enjoy finding grammatical errors and typos, please know that I have left a few of them in here for you!

Dedication

This book is dedicated to the memory of my grandparents, John and Grace Dexter, who were wonderful role models and two people who branded me with elements of good character.

Contents

Preface

This book endeavors to outline the elements of good character. It is my mission in this world of chaotic conditions to help our parents, teachers, daycare workers and preachers instill in all youth the elements contained within these pages. The training of our worlds' future leaders needs to begin at a very early age and continue throughout all the days of their lives. Parents MUST play a crucial role in equipping and branding their children with these elements of character.

Bad character is rampant all around us: in business, sports, entertainment and most notably with our elected officials. It is my opinion that a majority of the worlds' negative situations and products would not be in the condition that they are if our leaders lived by the elements of good character. Positive role models that live by the elements contained in these pages are becoming harder to find. This includes you parents reading this at home: you need to become role models for your children! What image are you going to brand upon your kids?

It is my hope that the following pages will inspire the hearts and minds of each of you. I pray that you will brand these elements of character not only in yourself, but in all of those whom you come in contact with. Remember – *a single thought, from a single person can change the world!*

- *Ken*

Acknowledgements

The guidance through the years from my parents, teachers, relatives and friends have all played a crucial role in getting these words onto paper. I thank each and every one of you: Bruce & Janet Owens, Tami & Russ Ashinger, Nicole Ashinger, Ryann Ashinger, Rachael Beutler, Michelle Matteson, Gail Hurt, April Braswell, Bill Hollabaugh, Terry Ryan, Kelly Jackson, Maggie Pringlemeir, Marge & Elliott Samson, Stefanie Zaks, Heather Samson, Barbara Silberberg, LaVaughn Mithen, Mildred Pirlot, Barbara Murray, Frank Bartoszewicz, Ellie Crowe, Wilma Arnott, Fran Richardson, Pamela Desvernine, Brenda Wittich, Candy & Bob Mason, Alejandro Tejas, Rod Russell, Wes Winters, Lavonia Criner, Judy Insley, Sherri Kleist, David & Dawn Baumunk, Jose Ortiz, Andres Ramirez, Steve & Trisha Chambers, Sandy Kuiper, Luciano Orozco, Richard Paguia, Arlene Bates, Barbara Winters, Carole Fishman, Carrie Proffitt, Bobby Hamman and Kit Smythe.

A special thanks to my mentors who I am so proud to call my friends: Shelley Stockwell, John Kirvan and Kevin Hogan.

Mary Millard, you are an amazing editor and skilled with a red pen! Thank you for your hours of proofreading.

Jennifer Battaglino, thank you for your contribution to this book. The foreword to a book is what sets the tone and prepares a reader for the upcoming pages and you did just that! It is a privilege to call you my friend and colleague.

Foreword by Jennifer Battaglino, LCSW

Small businesses do it. Large corporations do it. Product managers, service industries, and politicians do it. They brand themselves and their products every day. It's about achieving whatever their definition of success is, whether it's money or an election. Big business knows that the more they get us to *perceive* a positive image of their product the more likely we will buy it. Positive image equals the highest probability of success.

Early on in *Branding Your Character*, Ken Owens tells us, "Don't be blind to rumors until you have taken time to do the unbiased research to find the truth behind a product, person or business." He gives us the gift of how to do just that with all that follows – so take the time to get to know someone, dig a little deeper and educate yourself.

Ken brilliantly brings us to understand the concept of branding. He translates that knowledge into applicable positive character traits for us to strive for as individuals, teachers, students, friends, parents, professionals and peers, thus learning how to positively brand ourselves. Imagine having a life full of integrity, emulating who you want to be as a person and ultimately achieving success by navigating the world ethically.

Branding Your Character provides practical valuable information that you can start implementing today. It is interactive, engaging the reader to participate and take control of his or her life. Ken outlines the influences and components of our character, from relationships to faith to imagination. From exercises to thought-provoking questions, this book easily keeps your attention because you are turning the page wanting to know what comes next in the process. His holistic approach encompasses one's need for individuality, purpose and character. It is exciting to have a concise, articulate tool with which to work in my role as a psychotherapist. Teachers, therapists, family counselors, school guidance counselors, principals, social workers...the list is endless as to who will benefit from *Branding Your Character*.

And as the mother of three young children, I am delighted to be a part of such a positive message. This is a priceless opportunity to figure out the core values you want to develop for yourself or the children you are raising and teaching. Ken Owens helps us to analyze the people we respect and hone in on the traits we want to emulate. He provides the road map to developing a strong positive character, finding individuality and purpose while learning from both success and failure. To have a sense of self, be able to define who you are as an individual, and reach your true potential - who wouldn't want that for their children? It is truly inspiring...and possible.

To be blunt, it really doesn't matter how smart someone is if they can't convey the knowledge they possess with any efficacy. Ken Owens is an author who is articulate and makes his knowledge and experience accessible. We can all relate to his message and understand the process by which we can create a future of success for ourselves.

Character, Purpose, Individuality - since you have *Branding Your Character* in your possession, you are one giant step closer to achieving a great future.

- Jennifer Battaglino, LCSW
Larchmont, NY   USA

Jennifer Battaglino is a wife, mother and Clinic Director/Founder of The Harwood Group.   As a Licensed Psychotherapist, Jennifer's goal is to help clients find the emotional causes for their current concerns.   Once those problems are discovered she then begins to desensitize those issues, gain insight, and help her clients make positive cognitive changes.

Jennifer is one of the world's leading experts on Tinnitus (ringing of the ears).   She has worked with children and adults with Depression, Anxiety, Fears, Chronic Illnesses, as well as behavior modification for over a decade.

Along with her private practice, Jennifer also speaks at schools, conferences, conventions and seminars throughout the world.

Contact Jennifer: www.TheHarwoodGroupNY.com

Chapter 1

A Man's Character Is His Fate

> "*People grow through experience if they meet life honestly and courageously. This is how character is built.*" ~ Eleanor Roosevelt

We are about to embark on a journey of self-definition and discovery. A trek that will have us exploring core values which shape and mold a person into their true meaning. This will not be a religious exploration, but more importantly one filled with an inner sense of spiritual, philosophical and practical awareness. This journey will help to guide and define you into a positive and successful member of society.

This will not be an easy road to walk. Character is that silent elusive quality which our culture insists on, but is getting harder and harder to find. We look around our worldwide society and it is rare to find role models who exemplify good character for our youth to idolize. In many homes and businesses it is getting harder to find parents and leaders to instill these qualities in their children and employees. Turn on the news and we see politicians taking payoffs, parents being taken to jail, sports figures using drugs, clergy exposed in sexual scandals and business leaders purposely cheating the poor, elderly and hard working individuals.

Personal character at one time was one of the most fundamental issues in life, but that was before it started a downward spiral over the past few decades. What a person is in their inner-most self is their character, their true nakedness before their Creator. It is who you are when you are alone and the lights are off.

What is character? Merriam-Webster Dictionary defines character as:

> "1) one of the attributes or features that make up and distinguish an individual.
> 2) moral excellence and firmness."

Your character, your inner essence, shines through the best during the hardest times in your life. It takes many years of life and living for you to develop your character. It is not something that will just come to you from reading the pages of a book.

Character is found in people, within a corporate philosophy and in a product's traits. Character can come and go. We can have it one day, but then by greed and ego we lose it. It is much easier to keep it once we have it than it is to try and regain it if we lose it.

There is a big difference between reputation and character. Reputation is what others estimate, see, or think us to be, regardless of the validity of their judgment, while character is what one truly is. Through ignorance or malice or prejudice, a person may have a reputation that has been falsely imposed and one that has no connection to their true character. Although in some cases, it may be true that those assumptions which people put upon us are a representation of our true character, one must be ready to accept both positive and negative assumptions, and strive to correct or repair any false or negative reputation traits.

It is important to note that character formation and character appreciation are qualities that take time to grow and develop. That is why it is so important to begin instilling these qualities in our youth at an early age.

Let's use this analogy: think of your character as a freshly baked pie. The ingredients which you put into that pie - the flour, water, sugar and shortening - will determine the taste and outcome of the finished pie. Each of the qualities that we are going to discuss in this book are equal to the ingredients of that pie. Some ingredients are used more than others - two cups of flour versus a pinch of salt equates to a pinch of imagination blended with a whole bunch of faith. The individual ingredients are not equal in proportion, but each is an essential integral component to the successful outcome of the pie.

Before we can enjoy a taste of that pie, it first has to be baked in the oven under high heat. Likewise, before you can recognize your true perfection within yourself, you must endure a long period of failures and successes to hone your character. You have to be baked in the oven called *life*, forced under heat and pressure to bubble and blend each of the qualities which define your character.

A quick flash of monetary popularity is seen all around us and is not a basis of character: winning the lottery, hitting a jackpot in Las Vegas, a windfall inheritance, signing a new multi-year sports contract, etc. We must remember that these instances tend to be empty, unsatisfying, and deceiving to the elements of good character. It has been said, "many a person has come to moral starvation by feeding on the empty husks of popularity." Many times these empty flings with popularity are known to over-inflate the ego which leads to a negative shift in a person's character. We see this in sports when an athlete turns to drugs and sex, or in business when an executive turns to corruption and scamming customers.

I once knew an individual who won a $10 million lottery, but within a couple years was back to being broke. This person bought many material possessions and was proud of his flashy ego – however, he lacked the personal character to show charity or be wise enough to secure long term financial security for his family. Can you relate this story to someone you know or to a local business person, sports celebrity or politician in your area?

"Sow an act, and you reap a habit,
Sow a habit, and you reap a character,
Sow a character, and you reap a destiny."
~ G.D. Boardman

We grow a little every day, either for better or for worse. It is wise to ask yourself at the end of each day, "which did I do today?" Emerson said: "Mankind divides itself into two classes – Benefactors, one who does good toward another (good character) and Malefactors, one who does evil toward another (bad character)." If we belong to the latter, we turn our friends into enemies, make memory of pain, life a sorrow, the world a prison and death a terror. On the other hand, if we put one bright and good thought into anyone's mind, a smile on someone's face, one happy hour into a person's life, then we have done the work of an angel.

The word *character* is used in daily life in a very confusing and sometimes opposing manner. We say: "That is a person of character," meaning that they are one who has good character – a positive sense. Or we say with a shake of the head, chuckle in our voice or a shrug of the shoulders: "they are a character," meaning that they are peculiar, weird or sometimes even devious – a negative sense. In our discussion of character throughout this book we will only be using the context of the word in the positive sense.

The word *character*, strange as it may seem, is not found in the English version of the Bible, and yet religious educators have much to say about

23

character. Character formation within a cultural or religious context was a key component to living within a society and its importance cannot be overestimated - even though the word does not occur in Holy Texts. The closest translation to *character* is in the New Testament Greek version of Hebrews 1:3, where the word from which the English word *character* is derived occurs:

"God, who at sundry times and in diverse manners spake in time past unto the fathers by the prophets, hath in these last days spoken unto us by His son, whom He hath appointed heir of all things, by whom also he made the worlds; who being the brightness of his glory, and the **express image** of His person..."

Character has its origins to the phrase *express image* or *very image*. The Christian translation means that character or *very image* is the true expression of God's supreme love to man. If we further search into the derivative of *character*, we find more Greek roots that lead to the idea of engraving, cutting and stamping. By what we are, by our character, we engrave, carve or stamp (brand) ourselves upon our work, upon our environment and upon everyone with whom we come in contact. It is this impression of our lives that goes beyond time; it shares the deathless nature or immortality of the soul.

In a more metaphysical and spiritual sense, good character permeates your three-fold being and shines from within your body, mind and spirit. I believe that our spiritual essence is defined by our character, ethics, morals and beliefs. The world is full of many wonderful people, so why limit meeting them based on race, gender, sexuality, mannerisms, religion or age? Let an individual's character be the magnet which attracts or repels them, and not by one of these fore-mentioned prejudices.

One must take a holistic approach to character. Character education must be integrated into every part of your life. Your personal life, church life, business life, school life and your family life must all be touched by the effort to develop the positive core values that we will discuss in the upcoming pages.

We have all heard stories about the individual who is a devoted church-goer on Sunday mornings, shines with a smile to the congregation, but then goes home and beats the family and kicks the dog. Those people are not one's with character. You cannot develop a positive character by just passively attending a religious service. Character is an active participatory process which is developed over time!

One's character will, to a large extent, be what one chooses to make it. A philosophy supported by the title of this chapter is a quote from the Ancient Greek Philosopher Heraclitus: "A man's character is his fate." What is your fate in life? As you read these pages within this book, you may feel that you are approaching a fork in your life with two paths which lay ahead of you. One path will have you repeating the unfulfilled lessons from the past, while the other will have you implementing the lessons found here and growing into an enriched person whose fate will be a blessing to society.

"One thing is needful," says William Wordsworth:

"Money is not needful;
power is not needful;
cleverness is not needful;
but character alone –
a thoroughly cultivated will –
is that which can truly save us."

The development of character reminds me of an athlete in training for a big game. It takes years of training, practice, losses and wins to condition a great athlete to become their best. So too are those rules when they are applied to *you* in developing your character to live a prosperous, healthy and spiritual life. Your personal sense of character is not something that can be attained by inactivity and indifference. It is the result of a continual strenuous endeavor; it is a major life goal achievement.

Within the pages of this book, we will discuss six essential attributes of character which will brand you as an upstanding person. These individual elements, when brought together, produce a power which is greater than their sum parts: Individuality, Purpose, Imagination, Relationships, Work and Faith.

However, before we begin our exploration into these individual essential attributes, let us first take a look at the sub-groupings of important people within our lives who are responsible for instilling these six attributes within society's members.

Character Progression

Parents are the ones responsible for laying the foundation of good character early-on in their children's lives. In his book *The Four Agreements*, Don Miguel Ruiz enlightens us on how raising children is like training a dog. Both require a positive and nurturing environment which uses stimulus reinforcement to reward or punish the appropriate behaviors. Potty-training a child requires the same process as house-breaking a puppy.

The problem I see is the fact that many times parents themselves don't know how or what to do. We tend to pass on the traits with which we were raised. It takes education, and in some cases therapy too, for us to recognize and then overcome our shortcomings in order for us to be happy and successful. You can't teach your children something which wasn't taught to you.

I have the firm belief that parenting courses should be mandatory for raising a family. You can't drive a vehicle without taking classes and passing examinations. The same thing should be true for parents. I feel it would help us raise a generation of healthy and successful individuals whose lives are devoted to the betterment of themselves and society. Parents need to take responsibility for their actions and for the training and conditioning of their children.

The next group in line for instilling positive character traits within children is that of teachers. Teachers MUST recognize the importance they play in childhood development and the long term ramifications that continue into adulthood from what happens within their classrooms. Good teachers do the work of angels to inspire and uplift their students.

However, there are too many teachers who only show up in a classroom to collect a paycheck and who lack the ethical standards to recognize the damage that they are doing to their students. They have no sense of personal character and need to find other means of employment. Our entire worldwide society rests on the shoulders of those who educate our children – for our children are our future. All nations of the world need to empower their local governments to place a stronger emphasis on the importance of education.

Extended families, relatives and preachers are the next group which has an impact on the character development during youth. If someone within this group sees shortcomings in those around them, I empower you to intervene and assist to instill the positive elements we are discussing in this book. Character traits seem stronger in communal living households where the great-grandparents, grandparents, parents and children all reside within close proximity – or even under the same roof. A sense of shared responsibility for the successful development of the child seems evident. I share the same belief as what Hillary Clinton said:

28

"It takes a village to raise a child."

The last major group to have responsibility for character development is us – ourselves. We need to recognize as individuals our personal weaknesses and make the necessary changes to turn those weaknesses into strong positive traits. Even as young children growing into older adults, most have an innate sense to know right from wrong and good from bad; we need to listen to those inborn feelings, trust our intuition, and take responsibility for our own actions. Search out positive role models who are willing to be mentors. Educate yourself on those qualities which you are less familiar with – use this book as a guide. Don't be afraid to ask for assistance or guidance; asking others for help is a sign of strength – it's never a sign of weakness.

An ancillary group who has the power to shape character development includes: scout leaders, coaches, politicians and bosses - basically, anyone who has some form of power or direction over others. When you assume those roles of leadership, with it comes a sense of moral obligation to be of positive service to those under your direction. Contrary to that statement is the culture within many organizations who seemingly use and abuse their subordinates for their own power and advancement. It has been studied and documented that a decrease in morale and production occurs within those types of a dictatorship environment. People's inner drives for creativeness and motivation are fostered within a sharing group dynamic where open two-way communication is encouraged.

On a personal note, I still can name those teachers, relatives, scout leaders and family friends whom I feel had a positive impact on my life – even back to elementary school. Their names and faces are still clear in my mind. Some may not remember me to this day, but their words, actions and lessons shaped me for a lifetime. Who do you remember as those significant people who helped shape your current character traits?

A very important key to remember as you go through life is that you may not remember someone – but you never may know the impact which you had on their life – both positive and negative. A person living with the highest of character traits will always interact with people in a manner which will bring some level of happiness, peace, love and joy to those around them. How are you shaping the lives of those around you? We are all part of a larger society which can only grow healthier, stronger and more prosperous, when we as individuals choose to live our lives directed by peace, love and character.

So how does the title of this book and the act of branding fit into the realm of discussing character traits? Our next chapter will tie together the concepts of identity awareness (branding) for both businesses and individuals. That will then lay the framework for the rest of the chapters as we then embark on the journey to uncover six key character components to living a successful and dynamic life.

Author's Note: Feel free to use the pages of this book as a workbook and make notes in the margins. There are thought provoking questions in some chapters for you to answer along the way which will help to open up your awareness on this journey of character development and personal identity branding. Wherever possible, I tried to leave extra space for your notes so that all materials pertaining to this book are here on these pages.

Additional Resources

I have two great seminars which reflect the content of this chapter. Check out my website www.TheKenOwens.com for the programs on *Intelligence Parenting* and *Classroom Persuasion*.

Chapter 1 Diary Page:

Chapter 2

Leverage Your Brand

"Wise are those who learn that the bottom line doesn't always have to be their top priority."
~ William A. Ward

The buzz word in business, especially as it pertains to a product has been, and still is, that of *branding*. We hear it used in corporate identity, product development, sales, marketing, advertising and asset valuation. People talk all the time in boardrooms, TV newscasts and corporate cafeterias about this mystical sounding entity called *the brand*.

The Brand seems to be a creature unto itself, with a whole set of rules and upkeep separate from the corporation. This is quite similar to a publicly traded company whose stock values and trading is an entirely separate entity from the same corporation, and which may or may not have any direct correlation back to the financial stability or performance of the company (we'll talk more about this later).

Typically the word *branding* has only been used to describe the characteristics of a certain product. But the same principles are evident as well in a service industry. The service which you or your company offers is the direct equivalent to a product. Those same values which determine a product's brand recognition are the same values which determine a service's brand recognition; thus the determining factors for which a consumer will hire your plumbing services, landscaping services, house cleaning services or medical services over one of your competitors. A service's recognizable character traits will determine the overall success or failure of the service.

This thing known as *branding* is just as important to a sole-proprietorship business – either product or service based – as it is to a corporation of any size. I personally feel that it is even more important to an individual business owner because you do not have the luxury to hide behind the facade of a 'corporation'; the buck stops with you - the owner. You personally are the business, the brand, the decision-maker and the reputation of your business rests entirely on your shoulders.

Why do you think this concept of branding is so important in the context of a business setting (we will apply this same thinking to you as an individual in just a moment)? Well, like anything else, because there is BIG money associated with it. A top rated company can actually have a component (product or service) brand identity value worth more than the rest of the physical assets of their corporation. Let's get a better idea of what I am talking about.

2010 Brand Rankings in BILLIONS of Dollar ($) Valuation
Source: www.Interbrand.com

1.	Coca Cola	70.5
2.	IBM	64.7
3.	Microsoft	60.9
4.	Google	43.6
5.	GE	42.8
6.	McDonalds	33.6
7.	Intel	32.0
8.	Nokia	29.5
9.	Disney	28.7
10.	HP	26.9

So what does this listing represent? It means that the name Coca Cola, just the name with its feelings, identity and associated emotions, is worth $70,500,000,000! That price tag has nothing to do with the valuation of all the office buildings, machinery, factories, inventory, delivery trucks, raw ingredients, fork lifts, office equipment, etc. which are owned by the Coca Cola Corporation. That brand ranking valuation is just for the name *Coca Cola*.

Branding Through History

Many business schools and business book authors seem to tout this concept of branding as the newest, most important concept of a business. However, in reality, when we take a historical perspective, the process of branding and its associated meanings can be traced back many centuries.

Your 'family crest', which may date back to early medieval days, is exactly the same thing as the 'golden arches' are today to McDonald's Corporation. Your family crest was a symbol of the feelings, identity and emotions that others felt about your family when they saw your crest above your castle door, on tapestries hanging from the wall, scribed onto your stationary or forged into your battle armor.

The word branding in today's context, came from the concept of 'marking' something as ownership. The act of taking a hot iron and branding human slaves and livestock can also be found dating back many centuries. A recognizable logo (brand) was made from a piece of iron, placed in hot coals, and then burnt into the flesh of humans and animals. That easily recognizable mark (brand) was known to all around as to who the owner was of that property, similar to the 'mouse ears' that we see on all products which represent the Disney Corporation. We have certain feelings and emotions whenever we see that identifying brand; similar to a neighbor seeing a stray branded cow wandering the hills and knowing exactly who that cow belongs to. That stray cow with its brand will evoke certain emotions and feelings linking back to previous relationships with the neighbor who owns that cow.

Brands and branding can have both a positive and negative connotation. The image of your family crest can illicit positive emotions if your relatives were good, honest, sharing and caring, or it could illicit negative emotions if your relatives were known for pillaging the neighboring towns. Your stray branded cow found wandering the hillside might be returned to you if your neighbor likes you and has a good feeling toward you, or that cow could be on the dinner table in your neighbor's house if you are known to be a rotten or unfriendly person.

These same feelings occur everyday as you, the consumer, walk the aisles of your local grocery store, Walmart, Macy's or a car dealership. Interestingly, those same feelings occur everyday as you meet relatives, friends, neighbors, church members and other volunteers. We consciously and subconsciously brand other individuals based on our previous interactions with them. How many of you have felt that weird feeling in your stomach as you were sitting in the school or work cafeteria when that annoying co-worker or student sat down next to you? You say to yourself, "there goes my peaceful lunch because that other person never stops talking about their personal issues?" You have branded that person as a *pest*, based on your previous interactions with them.

Branding Perception

A positive or negative identity may or may not have any merit based on factual content. 99% of the time it is based on perspective and perception. For example, let's look at my hometown of Las Vegas. Whenever you hear the name Las Vegas, most people jump to the conclusion of casino gambling, drinking, prostitution and topless men's clubs. While some of those things occur in Las Vegas, it is not the only thing that Las Vegas has to offer. However, those are the emotions and feelings that this town has been 'branded' with from past publicity. Some people say they will never come here because of those identifying traits. But in reality, there is so much more which is missed from that type of judgmental attitude. Here is what I mean:

- Clark County, in which Las Vegas is based, does not allow prostitution; it is illegal here just like in most every other hometown. It is legal in surrounding counties, but it would take you an hour or two to drive to those famous 'ranches'.
- The beauty of Red Rock Canyon for a picnic and hiking is only 25 minutes west of the strip.
- Mt. Charleston has winter skiing and snowboarding on the mountain an hour north of the city.
- The immense beauty and wonder of the Hoover Dam and Lake Mead's water and boating activities is an hour east of the strip.
- Las Vegas is the entertainment capital of the world with every flavor of professional theatrical entertainment that you can imagine.
- The architecture of each of the resorts is a thing of beauty, with different themed adventures and world renowned artwork.

The point I am trying to make here is that a brand connotation may or may not be truly what you felt it was. I heard an advertisement somewhere on TV for a product which said, "An educated consumer is our best customer." The same thing holds true for brand identity – education is key. Don't blindly follow rumors or media reports until you have taken time to do unbiased research to find the truth behind a person, product, service or business. We have all heard stories about a person (usually negative), but then when we meet the person and get to know them, we typically find that none of those rumors were true and actually that person may have higher personal character traits than those spreading the negative rumors.

We react to everything in life based on our perspective, perception and emotional ties to that particular product, event or person. That is why the philosophy of branding for a product or service seems to be an entity within itself, much like the performance of a company's stock. Stocks will go up or down based on a stockholders perception and buyer's emotions which may have no basis to sound financial reasoning – look at the whole Bernie Madoff scandal. Bernie scammed billions of dollars out of people because he stirred a positive emotional 'smokescreen' which had no sound underlying financial basis; the same thing happens on Wall Street everyday. Bernie really 'Made-Off'! Actually, the study of stocks and trading is a perfect example of mass psychology, influence and persuasion.

Your Character = Your Personal Brand

So I bet by now you are asking yourself, "What does all this business and branding talk have to do with me as an individual person?" Well, those same qualities which have built the brand name of Coca Cola into a $70.5 billion dollar recognizable and enduring entity are the same fundamentals that you need to develop within yourself. How much do you think that your name, your character identity - your brand, is worth? Your character and the healthy positive (or sometimes negative) traits which you exhibit in your life are the measures by which others will brand and value you.

The goal of this book is to uncover positive character traits which you will implement into your life in order to grow into a positive, successful and healthy individual. Keep in mind what the opening quote of this chapter suggests: success comes in many forms besides just a financial focus. As a matter of fact, the more you focus on developing the topics within this book, and grow into a worldly positive person, the more financial success will be blessed upon you. By the time you are done reading this book, you will be able to implement the upcoming concepts and increase your personal brand valuation. You are a product – the outcome of your surroundings, parental conditioning, family and personal values, and the deeds you accomplish. Do you want your personal name recognition to have a positive brand image like Tylenol which helps millions of people per day, or do you want a negative brand image like Mr. Madoff as a scamming criminal? We as humans have free will and personal responsibility in our lives. This book will show you how to use your free will for the betterment of yourself and society – and how to define a successful life for yourself.

Your Next Steps

Please remember that the concepts and principles that we will be discussing within these pages can be applied to a product, a service, a corporation and to your sole proprietorship business - but also most importantly, to *you* as an individual. In business, once you start to focus your attention toward developing and enhancing the principles discussed here and not merely on a financial gain, you will then begin to see a return on your investment much higher than you dreamed possible. Likewise in your personal life, once you start to enrich your individual identity with the upcoming positive traits, many amazing opportunities will be presented to you.

As an individual, a parent, a teacher or anyone who molds the behaviors of others, remember that a blessed life is one fulfilled with integrity and ethics. In your personal life, it's not always about the bottom line dollar, career or material possessions – it's about how you conduct yourself on a daily basis and the amount of happiness and joy you bring into the lives of those around you.

There is an incredible journey which awaits those individuals who have the courage and determination to brand their life with positive character. The path on that journey is not easy. There will be concepts and exercises which will have you taking an honest look at yourself and reaching deep into your inner-being to define your true self. Things will change for you, for the better, as you allow yourself to grow into a healthy successful person branded with the highest of character traits.

It is okay to examine and question your relationship with yourself, your family, your friends and those whom you share your daily life with. Some of those relationships will grow stronger, while others will just need to drift away. Change is a good thing. Change is necessary. Change will allow you to make room for the new blessings which await you as you elevate your life on a higher existence – a life filled with character. The old saying, "out with the old and in with the new," is very appropriate at this moment.

For your optimum benefit, please take the time to complete the exercises within each chapter prior to moving on to the next chapter. Some of these questions build upon each other as you move to each upcoming chapter.

I want the best for you! *You* want the best for you! You *deserve* the best!

Chapter 2 Exercises:

1. Write down the words for the feelings, emotions and attitudes that you associate with these following people or businesses:

    *   Coca Cola

    *   Pepsi Cola

    *   Johnson Baby Shampoo

    *   Princess Diana

    *   Bill Gates

    *   Tom Cruise

    *   Walmart

    *   McDonald's

    *   Delta Air Lines

    *   Chase Bank

2. List five (5) people whom you know (family, friends, co-workers, etc.) that you feel exhibit the most positive of character traits which would reflect the highest level of a personal brand identity.

- Person 1 _____

- Person 2 _____

- Person 3 _____

- Person 4 _____

- Person 5 _____

3. Now it is time to be truly honest with yourself and do some deep inner soul searching for this question. Just like in question 1, write down the words for the feelings, emotions and attitudes that you sense other people associate with YOU! (How do others see your current character traits)?

4. From question 1, how can you relate the positive brand qualities for those ten items into character qualities for your personal life?

5. What kind of rumor mill gossip or negative judgments have you been branded with? Are any of those negative traits justified? Do you deserve it?

6. What can you do to repair any negative judgments about you?

Chapter 2 Diary Page:

Chapter 3

Never Follow The Crowd

"Follow your own star." ~ Dante

Human beings have an inherent curiosity in the finding, culture and development of manhood and womanhood to the highest possible degree. We are the only creatures who possess the tools and mindset to advance our society by each generation. Albeit, we see laziness and complacency rampant around us, but those poor souls are ignoring their 'inner sense' to reach their true potential. The prominent goal of the home, society and school needs to be that of helping to uncover and foster that inherent yearning within each person.

Schooling only develops what is already within an individual. Unfortunately, our educational institutions provide no courses in common sense, and training does not endow our youth with their own sense of self. Brilliant scholars make sorry work of everyday life because they lack the quality which we call 'common sense', and which is the rarest of talents to be found today. Education is only a tool with which to work in the world of thought and action, and everything depends on how well we use those tools.

Mother Nature has great respect for variety. No two leaves on a tree, no two flowers on a bush, no two cows in a herd, no two snowflakes and no two human fingerprints have been created identically alike. Each has its own individuality. Every person has their own separate and distinct personality, and this law of nature must be recognized in all effective educational methods. Those parents or teachers who do not individualize their child or student fails in a large measure during the adventure called education.

The home and the school should enable all youth to find themselves and discover their special individuality, in order that each may follow their true potential, their own star, with courage and purpose. An individual should be more than a mere puppet, carbon-copy or imitator of the rest of the group.

In this fast-paced computer age, there is great danger of losing our individuality. Here are some pertinent words of wisdom from a great historical educator and former President of the United States. Even though these words were written in the early 1900's, it is amazing how true they still are today. In the 20th century Woodrow Wilson wrote:

"The law tries nowadays to deal with men in groups and companies, to punish them as corporate wholes. It is an idle undertaking. It will never be successfully accomplished. The only responsibility to which human society has ever responded, or ever will respond, is the responsibility of the individual. The law must find the individual in the modern corporation and apply its demands and its punishments to him if we are to check any of the vital abuses which now trouble the business world. You may pile fines ever so high in the public treasury, and corporations will still continue to do things that they should not do, unless you check them by taking hold of individuals who are ultimately responsible for their policy."

The recent actions of corporations like Enron, Halliburton, the banking and mortgage businesses, the accounting firm scandals and the BP oil spill surely bring light to those words in this 21st century environment. Our government leaders need to enforce those words of Mr. Wilson based on the current business indiscretions. However, that is another problem – most elected officials themselves lack a sense of individual character.

Mr. Wilson continues:

"Every great age of the world of which I have ever heard, was an age not characterized chiefly by cooperative effort, but characterized chiefly by the initiative of indomitable individuals. You cannot give an age distinction by the things that everybody does. Each age derives its distinction from the things that individuals choose to be singular in doing of their own choice. Every turning point in the history of mankind has pivoted upon the choice of an individual, when some spirit that would not be dominated stood tall in its independence and said: 'I go this way. Let any man go another way who pleases.'"

There are numerous notable historic figures that represent this statement: Jesus, Buddha, Gandhi, Mother Teresa, Nelson Mandela, Martin Luther King Jr. and Rosa Parks to name just a few. Each of their individuality of action and true purpose changed the course of time.

As we saw on December 1, 1955 with Rosa Parks, disobedience is one of the conditions to foster change. Her unwillingness to give up her seat to a white passenger is marked in history as the beginning of the modern day civil rights movement in the United States. Her disobedience changed the course of time.

As we look back through time, what would have been the effect of implicit obedience? In many scenarios that is a very frightening thought, especially when we look at certain events or people like Hitler. We owe a debt of gratitude to those disobedient individuals whose individuality of action has forged new paths through history. Their legacy lives on! What paths are you forging and what kind of legacy are you going to leave?

We live in an age of conformity. Unfortunately, it is a time when everybody goes about seeking to say what everyone else is saying, while dressing and looking like everyone else. We see this most prevalent in schools where children try to mimic each other in order to be 'hip' and 'cool' while trying to 'fit in'. Even worse is when they wear certain clothing or colors to signify a gang affiliation.

I know of one school district in Arizona which has mandatory uniform policies within all grade levels that has helped to deter violence in their district. There are two sides to that kind of policy as it pertains to this book. On one hand it keeps all students on the same socio-economic level – expensive and designer apparel is not permitted thus richer children cannot taunt and tease poorer students over clothing, jewelry, etc. Plus, it reduces the chances of students showing any gang color affiliations. However, as we have been discussing here in this chapter, it may take away from the student's sense of individuality. But hopefully, this lays an even playing field to foster a better educational environment thus allowing for increased scholastic awareness and also allowing students to develop their individuality based on their personalities instead of clothing and other materialistic items.

School-age children are under many pressures. We can all remember the tormenting and teasing over many issues as each of us went to kindergarten through high school graduation. Parents need to encourage communication from their children as to the daily events occurring within school. They should also volunteer and be active participants on school committees in order to keep a keen eye on the activities within the school district.

This type of communication includes getting back to old-time dinner table conversations. On a recent episode of the reality TV show *Khloe and Lamar*, Khloe Kardashian commented on how she remembered nightly dinner table conversations and how important they were to her upbringing. Everyone at their family table had to discuss both their high and low points of that day. I was impressed to hear such a heartfelt comment from Khloe.

Always remember to be yourself in what you say and do – and teach that to your children! Let your life be the best expression of your unique individuality, your cultured and educated personality. It is a bold and splendid thing to stand out and say, "I will not be a pawn to the marketing media or group pressures".

Wilson also suggested:

"I will not bow down to the weak habit of pursuing everything that is popular, everything that belongs to the society to which I belong. I will insist on telling society, if I think it so, that in certain fundamental principles it is wrong; but I will not be fool enough to insist that it adopt my program at once for putting it right. What you should insist upon is speaking the full truth to it and never letting it forget the truth, speaking and living the truth again and again and again."

Wilson refers to this motivated individual as a *persistent personality*. A persistent individual is not a defiant individual, not an impractical individual, but an individual who does try, who cannot be ashamed, and cannot be silenced. They are a person who tries to observe the fair manner and bring light to the unfair. Even though vast diversity is represented through individuality, we all need to be accepting of the opinions of others.

Wilson also observed almost a century ago:

"In our public school life there is often the danger of losing our individual characteristics, and the danger of failing to develop our separate personalities. In our large and growing schools there is the tendency to standardize the courses of study for the majority, and fail to provide for the special needs of the minority. The personal touch and interest of the teacher are important factors in the culture of personality. The school and the teacher that can provide for the individual development of the largest number of students are most successful."

Woodrow Wilson wrote those words decades ago and just look at how truly they reflect our present day education system! To be like another person or group of people robs us of the opportunity to be ourselves. We see this rampant mimicking in most classroom settings. We need to empower our educators to develop a personal initiative backed by much thought, much determination and much individualized care, to focus on the students as individuals and not part of a mass herd (gang mentality).

One of the many continuing failures in the educational system is the concept that everyone MUST learn in the same modality. That method of teaching is the standard verbal mode of instruction, thus forcing everyone to conform to classroom

53

standards which only address the educational needs of the median range, and which perpetrates the herd gang mentality.

In 1983, Howard Gardner published his new philosophy of the *Multiple Intelligence Theory* which goes a long way to help foster individuality. This new concept was meant to show that not everyone learns the same way. Each person has qualities which are learned and exhibited in multiple modalities, and the individuality of each person must be recognized. Not everyone can learn at the same rate from archaic verbal instruction. Here's what Gardner maintains as the eight multiple ways (intelligences) on how we learn:

Bodily-kinesthetic – Physical, bodily movement, physiology, acting and performing reflect this modality.

Interpersonal – Refers to interaction with others. These people tend to be extroverts.

Verbal-linguistic – This is the current main mode of learning: words, languages, writing, speech, listening to lectures.

Logical-mathematical – Reasoning, logic, numbers, computers and mathematics all define this intelligence.

Intrapersonal – This is a high recognition of personal feelings, motivations, and emotions, and tends to be introverted.

Visual-spatial – This has to do with your spatial surroundings and vision. It is the ability to visually assemble objects, such as puzzles.

Musical – Refers to learning from rhythm, pitch, tone, and music.

Naturalistic – Added to the list in 1997. Refers to learning from nature and its surroundings and being outdoors with influences from animals and weather.

An effective teacher, preacher, salesperson or corporate trainer must include as many of these intelligence modalities into their presentations as possible for increased audience comprehension. This also helps to disperse the herd learning and empower individuals in educational and business settings. There are several studies which have shown that comprehension is increased if there is a physical activity associated with the learning activity, such as: listening to books on tape while driving or exercising, or writing notes while listening to a lecture. Try to incorporate two or three of these modalities into your next program and test this strategy within your own setting.

There are many more great pioneers of thought and action who have dared to be different besides the ones already noted. A few others are: Thomas A. Edison, Booker T. Washington, Susan B. Anthony, Charles A. Lindbergh, Henry Ford, Ray Croc, Whoopi Goldberg, Valentina Tereshkova, Walt Disney, Barbara Walters, Katherine Graham and Bill Gates. These individuals had the courage of their convictions that moved them forward through adversity to attain notable achievements and advance our society as a whole. They did more than equal the success of their predecessors, for they stood on the shoulders of those preceding them and used them as a springboard to reach new heights.

In today's age of a global world society, we need more men and women who are alert free-thinkers with an abundance of common sense. There are many problems facing our worldwide society which need innovative and challenging solutions, and it is essential that all women and men take the lessons learned from the noted individuals mentioned in this as well as the upcoming chapters. The work of the world that is really worthwhile must be mixed with individuality of thought and a directed sense of purpose – a persistent personality. Men and women with innovation, focus, determination and individuality of will are needed today more than ever.

Individuality of thought is a liberating movement. Set your mind on things that are above and beyond you – for where the thoughts go, the soul climbs.

Chapter 3 Scientific Case Study

Who we are and who we want to be are two very big questions that can bring opposing answers. They are questions that I hope this book will help to bring some clarity of purpose for you. In order for one to mesh those two questions into a clear focus, we need to have a heightened sense of awareness of who we are as an individual.

Timothy D. Wilson, a psychologist from the University of Virginia, offers us a few ways to better know ourselves from an article in *Perspectives on Psychological Science*. "Self-knowledge is less a matter of careful introspection than of becoming an excellent observer of oneself," says Wilson. He has expanded his studies from the standard emotions, personality and attitudes to also include past feelings, future wants and predicting future feelings. His philosophy states it is just as important to know who we were and who we will be, as it is knowing who we are today.

This power of self-knowledge is a drive that motivates us on our path of individuality. The deeper we know ourselves the more comfortable we will be, with ourselves and those around us. Current research and medical science, like the invention of the fMRI, has led to a deeper discovery of the bio-mechanics of human behavior, and is moving the field of psychology to new levels. We all need to continue the study of *self*, along with keeping abreast of emerging new research which will help us answer those internal questions.

Chapter 3 Quotes For Thought:

"The individual has always had to struggle to keep from being overwhelmed by the tribe. If you try it, you will be lonely often, and sometimes frightened. But no price is too high to pay for the privilege of owning yourself."
~ Friedrich Nietzsche

"You are the child of the universe, no less than the trees and the stars; you have the right to be here. And whether or not it is clear to you, no doubt the universe is unfolding as it should." ~ Desiderata

"Our essential nature is uncreated, never-born, and free in and for itself. It is found in all creatures, but is not restricted to them; it is outside all creatures, but not excluded from them." ~ The Cloud of Unknowing

"Be the change you wish to see..." ~ Gandhi

"Everything without tells the individual that he is nothing; everything within persuades him that he is everything."
~ X. Doudan

"I am not here to please other people or to live my life their way. I am here to learn how to love myself and to love other people unconditionally." ~ Louise Hay

Chapter 3 Exercises:

1. What traits do you feel are your strongest as an individual?

2. List one or two times when you have strayed away from group belief and stood your ground as an individual? How did it feel? Was your point/opinion recognized?

3. Have you been involved in a group/gang scenario that had negative implications to your self worth? How did that make you feel?

4. Who was your favorite teacher(s)? What qualities made them your favorite? How did they inspire you?

Chapter 3 Diary Page:

Chapter 4

The Purpose of Life is A Life of Purpose

> "The only thing that stands between a person and what they want from life is merely the will to try it and the faith to believe it is possible."
> ~ Richard M. DeVos

A prerequisite for having a positive character is having a purpose. One should determine at the very outset to make something of oneself. There is an explosive power in a purposeful person which is essential to self worth and success. To have such a purpose does not mean the growth of an unchangeable will, because a wise person will change their mind on occasions but a fool never does. Your purpose is the aim toward which you work in the effort to live a successful life.

To live without purpose is like going on a journey without first deciding where to go. Don't be like the woodworker when asked what he was making, responded, "It may be a statue or it may be a bedpost." Know your purpose before you begin your project. Your purpose is your roadmap, it's your blueprint; it gives you focus and direction, and is the power which keeps you on your path of living a life of character. Without purpose, a person becomes an aimless drifter and achieves nothing. A person filled with purpose is like an architect who works toward an ideal which he hopes to see realized in actual wood, stone, glass and metal. Those materials which an architect uses - the wood, stone, glass and metal - to someone not familiar with the construction industry may seem unrelated and a confusing mess; however, when the plan of the architect falls in line, everything takes its proper shape in order to make the initial vision a finished reality. That initial vision was the architect's purpose for that particular project.

The word purpose traces its roots back to the 13th century French word *porpos*, meaning 'aim, intention, to put forth'. There are many other words you can use that imply the somewhat-same meaning for our discussions here: aim, intention, goal, mission, objective, reason, direction, ambition and resolve to name a few. However, for me, *purpose* packs more punch to the meaning as it deals with our character.

Some say that the word *intent* can also be used synonymous with purpose, but I disagree. To me, intent is the energy and the power that you put forth behind your purpose. Your intentions can make just about anything be either negative or positive, just like purpose, as we will examine a bit later. For example, a gun is a neutral item and it is the intention of the user which makes it negative (kill another person), or positive (hunt for food). If your purpose is to be a computer programmer, then your good intention will be to develop new software programs to help society; or if you have bad intentions, then you develop trojans and viruses which negatively harm society. See the difference in meaning? Most things in life are neutral, but it is the act of you applying your intention which then makes it negative or positive. It is my goal for each of you to develop your lives in the most positive and loving of intentions.

The premise for the smash Broadway hit musical *Avenue Q* has the lead character trying to find meaning and purpose in life (music and lyrics by Robert Lopez and Jeff Marx). Although a play with some adult content, the underlying message is very meaningful:

> "Purpose,
> It's that little flame
> That lights a fire…
> I don't know where
> I'm gonna look,
> But I'm gonna find
> My PURPOSE
> Gotta find out
> Don't wanna wait!
> Got to make sure that my
> Life will be great!
> Gotta find my purpose
> Before it's too LATE."

The cast does find purpose to life and it is summed up in two little words - helping others. Those two little words carry a great amount of weight and responsibility toward directing one's life.

Many centuries ago, King Philip of Macedonia was entertaining several Persian ambassadors at his palace, with his young son, the prince, a very interested spectator. Soon, the prince's shyness faded away and he began to talk freely with the visitors who had traveled such a great distance. The prince asked the Persian ambassadors a great many questions; the ambassadors were very interested in the boy because his questions were wise and thoughtful. The prince asked them how far they had traveled, the size of their country, the nature of the roads on which they journeyed, and how they had managed to navigate the high country of Asia. He asked them about their king, about his power, and about the kind of power their people possessed. The young prince wanted to know what their king did with his enemies when he had captured them in war. The boy was named Alexander, later to be known as *the Great*, the conqueror of Persia and the world. Even at such a young age, Alexander the boy was showing what he would be when he became Alexander the Great. It was the power of purpose, which shaped his character and determined his future in world history.

You too, no matter what age you are now, can harness that same power, define your purpose, and become Great! It's never too late to go back to school, start your own business or change jobs. Don't let excuses hold you back - look within yourself and let your true inner purpose be your guide.

Be like Nola Ochs, who in 2007, became the world's oldest college graduate at the age of 95. Do you know what she wanted to do after she received her diploma in History? "I plan to seek employment on a cruise ship, going around the world as a storyteller," she said. There is also George Brunstad, who at 70 years old became the oldest person to swim the 21 miles across the English Channel. These two examples could have used a multitude of excuses – age, prior failures, previous success, or a million others to deter them from their purpose, but they didn't. Let these two examples be a motivation for all of us! What kind of example can you set to be a motivating force to those around you?

You as a parent must instill that same vision of purpose into your children. They do not need to be born of royal blood like the young Alexander to be educated within the same methodology of a prince or princess. If you empower them and treat them as the precious gems they are they will grow into their own true greatness. Perhaps not to conquer the world like Alexander the Great, but you will have instilled in them the purpose and confidence to conquer all of their dreams, goals and desires.

The ideal of purpose has been discussed and debated for centuries. From Philosophers to Psychologists, many have put their own slant to the importance of purpose in ones' life. Noted psychiatrist Victor Frankl's summarizations say that, "man's search for meaning (or in other words, man's purpose), is the primary motivation for life." Fankl's terminology of 'search for meaning' is the same as Sigmund Freud's 'will (search) for pleasure', which is synonymous with Friedrich Nietzsche's 'will to power'.

This supports each of their differing views on the importance of purpose in life – meaning vs. pleasure vs. power. Ayn Rand put forth the notion that purpose is one of the three ruling values of human life. As we have grown as a society over the years, I tend to believe that purpose is becoming a more significant component to our lives.

James Allen was an African-American photographer who owned a studio in Harlem between World Wars I and II. His works were extremely popular and frequently reproduced in numerous periodicals. He was one of the very few black photographers of his time to be recognized as a true artist. Allen's following quote is important to our study of purpose:

"A man should conceive of a legitimate purpose in his heart, and set out to accomplish it. He should make this purpose the centralizing point of his thoughts. It may take the form of a spiritual ideal, or it may be a worldly object, according to his nature at the time being; but whichever it is, he should steadily focus his thought forces upon the object which he has set before him. He should make this purpose his supreme duty, and should devote himself to its attainment, not allowing his thoughts to wander away into ephemeral fancies, longings, and imaginings. This is the royal road to self-control and true concentration of thought. Even if he fails again and again to accomplish his purpose (as he necessarily must until weakness is overcome), the strength of character gained will be the measure of his true success, and this will form a new starting point for future power and triumph."

With words as poetic and insightful as those, James Allen was much more than an Artist-Photographer. He was a philosopher and a man of character who understood the importance of having a purpose in life; of having a drive, a determination and an aim to guide and direct all actions of life. Allen's character glistened in each of his photographs. When you are living a purposeful life, your character can be seen in all that you do.

Those very powerful words distinctly summarize my feelings as to the importance of purpose. To me, purpose means everything. Purpose is the underlying goal which determines all that we do. Do you have a positive purpose – to be of service to others, to advance an ideal, or maybe to bring joy and happiness to others? Or do you have a negative purpose – to bring no meaning to society, to be a welfare recipient, or to bring harm and discomfort to others?

Once you decide if you are going to pursue a life of positive or negative purpose, then there are careers which you can investigate. For example:

> Negative purpose careers: bum, prostitute, no job, drug dealer, con artist, career criminal, computer spammer and a host of others.

> Positive purpose careers: teacher, minister, police, fire, doctor, nurse, salesperson, garbage collector, good parent, construction worker, factory worker, waiter/waitress, business owner and a host of others.

As an individual you need to have purpose to guide you toward your goals. In a business setting, your company has to have an inherent sense of purpose as well. Just like an individual, a business can have a negative purpose (fraudulent mortgage company, selling unfit used cars, your toxic waste polluting the community, using inferior ingredients in your products and many more). Or your business can have a positive purpose (building energy efficient products, manufacturing life saving devices and implants, a lawn or maid service, or any others that have goodwill toward society and being of helpful service to others).

The smash Broadway Hit Musical *Wicked* (Stephen Schwartz, Winnie Holzman, and Gregory Maguire), has a song sung by the Wizard which supports our discussion here of purpose. The Wizard proclaims that all through history, "A man has been a traitor or a liberator, a rich man a philanthropist or a thief. And one could be a crusader or a ruthless invader." We see how the lyrics from this song are the direct perception of negative purpose vs. positive purpose.

Within the realm of religion, purpose has been widely debated for centuries. The New Testament in the Bible states: "And we know that all things work together for good to them that love God, to them who are the called according to his purpose (Rom 8:28)." Many use the words 'mission' and 'calling' in the religious context to denote purpose.

Christian writer Rick Warren's best-selling book *Purpose Driven Life* supports the notion that God is the one whom inherently instills into everyone their predestined purpose in life. For many devoted Christian followers who believe those teachings, more power to them. If that is the mechanism which gets a person to grasp onto the meaning and power for a directed purpose, then I support that.

I, however, take a different view on the religious aspect of purpose. I share more of an esoteric spiritual view on purpose versus the hard core religious belief. I wholeheartedly believe that recognizing your true purpose is not only essential to having good character, but it is essential to life itself. Your purpose should be the reason why you wake up and conquer each day.

I believe in a higher power. Some religions call that power God, Allah, Mohammed, Yahweh, Elohim or even Goddess, but I also believe that we as human beings are the only creatures to be instilled with free will and personal responsibility from that higher power. We as individuals have the free will to choose, nurture and defend our own purpose. It is then our personal responsibility to accept the consequences of our choice. If we choose a negative purpose of crime, then we accept the time we will spend locked in jail. If we choose a positive purpose to be a doctor, then we accept the years of college and long work days away from family.

All religious and spiritual philosophies only promote goodness, well-being and a positive purpose. Being of service to others is the greatest purpose one can aspire to achieve. Therefore, no one should judge the differences in positive life purposes – a small business owner is just as important as a corporate CEO, a trash collector just as important as a brain surgeon, an author/speaker just as important as a kindergarten teacher, and a stay-at-home parent just as important as a firefighter. All positive purpose individuals need to co-exist in order to maintain a productive society.

The two biggest questions asked by nearly everyone in religious houses around the world are:

- What am I supposed to do?
- Why am I here?

Both of those questions revolve around discovering your purpose. Their answers lie not only within each of us, but also within the framework of your personal religious/spiritual context.

It often costs a great deal to maintain the ideals of a positive purpose. Unending hard and continuous work is the price you need to pay for the achievement of a worthwhile purpose. Andrew Carnegie spent 18 years of his life to accumulate his first $1000 of capital. Abraham Lincoln failed twice to become a US Senator before he became elected as the 16th President of the United States. Thomas Edison failed over 1000 times before inventing the first light bulb. Soichiro Honda, Founder of the Honda Motor Company, stated, "Success is 99 percent failure." But keep in mind - it is the drive of your purpose which keeps you going, again and again and again. With odds such as that, we need to live by the motto "fail your way to success."

Basketball superstar Michael Jordan wasn't good enough and was cut from his high school basketball team in his sophomore year, even though he felt deep within that basketball was his calling. Jordan turned his initial failure into the motivating force to practice hour after hour on the court. After becoming a superstar, Jordan was asked what was the driving force that changed for him in high school? Jordan replied, "Whenever I was working out and got tired and figured I ought to stop, I'd close my eyes and see that list in the locker room without my name on it; that usually got me going again."

The likes of Albert Einstein, Michael Jordan, Winston Churchill, Carnegie, Lincoln and Edison failed miserably in their lives, and yet they are known not for their failures but for their eventual amazing successes. That time of seeming failure is really a period of preparation during which the qualities (character) of real success are developed and strengthened. When the critical hour arrives, the person with a purpose who has been schooled and disciplined in the qualities we are discussing in this book will surely win! The path of purpose is the path of duty and service, which is a path not easy to travel but pays a great dividend in good character.

All of us are ordinary when we are born. Some of us will be extraordinary when we die. It's your purpose in life which will determine if you will become one of the extraordinary!

Chapter 4 Scientific Case Study

Patricia A. Boyle, PhD and her fellow researchers at Rush University Medical Center have found that older adults who possess a greater purpose in life have lower mortality rates. Boyle states, "Purpose in life reflects the tendency to derive meaning from life's experiences and be focused and intentional." She further goes on, "The finding that purpose in life is related to longevity in older persons suggests that aspects of human flourishing – particularly the tendency to derive meaning from life's experiences and possess a sense of intentionality and goal-directedness - contribute to successful aging. Although we think that having a sense of purpose in life is important across the lifespan, measurement of purpose in life in older persons in particular may reveal an enduring sense of meaningfulness and intentionality in life that somehow provides a buffer against negative health outcomes."

The researchers were excited about these findings because it lends some scientific support to the message that many self-help books, preachers, and psychologists have been saying for centuries. If this research has that kind of impact in elderly people, just think how powerful it will be in the lives of children, and the benefits they will endure as they grow into purposeful mature adults.

Chapter 4 Quotes For Thought:

"Great minds have purposes, others have wishes."
~ Washington Irving

"Great ambition is the passion of a great character. Those
endowed with it may perform very good or very bad acts.
All depends on the principles which direct them."
~ Napoleon Bonaparte

"To put away aimlessness and weakness, and to begin to
think with purpose, is to enter the ranks of those strong
ones who only recognize failure as one of the pathways to
attainment; who make all conditions serve them, and who
think strongly, attempt fearlessly, and accomplish
masterfully." ~ James Allen

"What allows us, as human beings, to psychologically
survive life on earth, with all of its pain, drama, and
challenges, is a sense of purpose and meaning."
~ Barbara De Angelis

"Happiness comes from fidelity to a worthy purpose."
~ Helen Keller

"If your heart is straight with God, then every creature will
appear to you as a mirror of life and a sacred scripture.
No creature is so small and insignificant so as not to
express and demonstrate the goodness of God."
~ Thomas A. Kempis

Chapter 4 Exercises:

1. Have you determined your purpose yet? If so, what is it?

2. If not, take a few minutes to write down a couple choices. By the end of this book, come back and revisit what you have listed here.

3. How many failures have you had in your life? How have they made you stronger?

4. What lessons have you learned from each of those failures in question 3 that, in the end, had positive effects on you?

5. What are your personal beliefs as far as your purpose being instilled within you from a higher source vs. you having free will and personal responsibility?

Chapter 4 Diary Page:

Chapter 5

Imagination Is More Important Than Knowledge

"The soul never thinks without a mental image."
~ Aristotle

The next essential element of character is that of imagination - the picturing power of the mind, a constructive and creative energy.   Nothing seems more elusive, when we try to appreciate it, than the element of imagination. It is the creative element of the mind in everything we do - whether it is the scientist, poet, painter, computer programmer, astronaut or the religious prophet.

By the power of imagination, the architect sees the completed skyscraper or cathedral long before the ground is broken or the foundations are laid. The sculptor, by her imagination, sees the exquisite completed statue in the rough block of marble long before the first chisel strikes that piece of rock. The engineers who planned the construction of the Panama Canal thus visualized its locks and waterway years before its completion, as did the worldwide collection of scientists who designed the International Space Station.

If you take a moment to reflect back on the various achievements in your life, you too will trace the completed task back to an initial spark of imagination. As we further discuss the element of imagination, we will see that it is a powerful energetic force which must be reckoned with and is crucial in branding your character. The force of imagination is often strong enough to enable a person to overcome all the circumstances in their surroundings and rise up to conquer their goals.

The power of imagination can make a well man ill and an ill man well. Over the past couple decades, physicians have finally recognized the positive influence which imagination has on the healing process. The famed Mayo Clinic has recently joined the list of supporters who now give credibility to what Aristotle and Hippocrates taught many centuries ago – that positive images in the brain can enliven the heart and body.

In a published edition of the *Mayo Clinic Health Letter*, they stated that guided imagery (positive imagination) has been shown to help patients in these major areas:

- Reducing side effects from cancer treatment.
- Reducing fear and anxiety prior to surgery. Studies have shown that surgery patients who participated in two to four guided imagery sessions required less pain medication and left the hospital more quickly than those who hadn't used imagery.
- Managing stress.

- Managing headaches. Studies have shown that guided imagery may aid in reducing the frequency of migraine headaches as effectively as taking preventive medications.

Several hospitals are now employing Hypnotherapists, Massage Therapists and Ministers who help a patient tap into their mind-power to assist with their imagination for enhanced healing.

In a persuasion setting: the most successful doctor is one who possesses the ability to inspire their patient's confidence in them, and then in the course of treatment which will be administered. The same holds true in a business sales setting: the most successful sales people are those who can inspire their client's confidence that their product or service is the best solution for that client, even if it comes at a higher price tag than that of a competitor. That ability to inspire as mentioned in these two examples is the ability to tap into the imagination of the other person and have them paint a mind-picture of the positive outcome which you are trying to invoke.

There was a story told in the early 1900's in *The Psychological Review* about an experiment conducted by Mr. Slossen which showed how easily it is to invoke the power of imagination:

During the course of his lecture, Mr. Slossen presented to his audience a glass bottle, which he uncorked with elaborate precautions; then, with stopwatch in hand, asked the audience to indicate the exact moment at which the nasty odor could be smelled. Within fifteen seconds those in the front rows held up their arms, and within forty seconds those at the other end of the room indicated that the nasty odor had reached them. There was a steadfast minority in the room who blatantly argued that there was not any detectable odor. Mr. Slossen believes that many more would have finally smelled the odor if he hadn't ended the experiment after only a minute because several people in the front row were leaving the room due to becoming physically ill. The interesting point to this experiment is the fact that the glass bottle merely contained pure distilled water.

That is one very powerful experiment which shows the power of imagination. This example is very pertinent to me as well; I use an experiment similar to this with a lemon in the opening of my comedy hypnosis stage show. I hold up a wax lemon, which looks very real, and tell the audience: "See this lemon in my hand, now close your eyes and visualize that lemon which I am holding – see its bright yellow color. Smell the fragrant lemon juice as I take a knife and cut that lemon in half. Now, taste that bitter lemon juice as I squeeze it on your tongue." It's at that point when the audience members pucker their mouths, they start salivating, and most will have watery eyes. This is a powerful example that I use to show the power of imagination where you can actually see, smell and taste using guided imagery. It is those people who have the most dynamic response to this exercise who may make the best participants on stage in my comedy hypnosis show.

It has been said that the best speakers and writers are those who speak and write imaginatively. By this, it is not meant they scam or lie but can tell a story in an imaginative way. No one knows this better than an author of fiction stories. The power of those stories rest in the fact that people feel intuitively that the characters portrayed on those pages have a true, real personality. I don't care if it is romance novels, science fiction stories, or historical accounts such as Harriet Beecher Stowe's *Uncle Tom's Cabin;* it is the same imaginative power. The words are read from the pages of those books, but spring to life within the imagination of the reader.

Mark Johnson says in his book *The Body in the Mind:*

"Without imagination, nothing in the world could be meaningful. Without imagination, we could never make sense of our experience. Without imagination, we could never reason toward knowledge of reality."

I heard a story once about Einstein's Theory $E=MC^2$, that it actually came to him in a dream. If this was the case, then it upholds Mark Johnson's statement and shows that imagination can actually foster the growth of knowledge and reality.

Our sleep dreams and our waking day dreams are both manifestations of our imagination. Many parents and teachers seem to deter children from having an active imagination and scold them if they daydream. Much of this stems back to the 1950's and prior when daydreams were thought to be the sign of laziness or even much worse – neurosis and psychosis. However, much study has been done since then and brain scans with fMRI technology actually shows the opposite – that daydreaming is a healthy creative process which helps people sort through problems and achieve success.

British Therapist Dan Jones studied the patterns and thinking styles of successful people like Richard Branson, Albert Einstein, Leonardo da Vinci and Walt Disney. He found that through the centuries, they all had one thing in common – they each spent time daydreaming about their successes. Each of us needs a supportive environment to foster our daydreams and allow our minds to tap into that inner creative imagination process so that we may achieve our individual successes.

The element of imagination is not new. Its importance has been discussed for many centuries. The current word *imagination* can be traced back to two roots:

> Greek word - *phantasia*
> Latin word - *imaginatio*

Many centuries of study into imagination and mental dynamics can be traced back to Ancient Greek and Roman times, and Aristotle (384 BC-322 BC) seems to be the founding researcher into these topics. His viewpoint was, "Imagination is the process by which we say that an image is presented to us." Through the ages, imagination has been associated with those things that are not actually in our current reality, things that are not really there. Over the centuries, many philosophers, metaphysicians and scientific minds have debated the existence, power and importance of imagination. There are far too many differing views to discuss here, but some of the most prominent names for further research have been: Descartes, Hume, Philostratus, Coleridge, Sartre, Ryle, Frege, Watson, Paivio and Kosslyn, to name just a few.

In esoteric spiritual teachings, there is a Universal Natural Law which states: "Thoughts are things and energy follows thoughts." Meaning, your thoughts and your imagination may evolve into reality. Your thoughts and your imagination can come true because the universe will send energy to those thoughts in order to manifest your imagination and your dreams. There have been thousands of self-help books and workshops written which all can be distilled down to this one universal axiom – thoughts are things and energy can bring those thoughts into manifestation. This esoteric viewpoint has been support by the writings of Scottish Philosopher Dave Hume (1711-1776), whose belief was, "Nothing we imagine is absolutely impossible." Meaning whatever is imaginable is possible, and vice versa - if something is impossible it also has to be unimaginable.

The whole movement of *The Secret* revolves around this spiritual principle. The Law of Attraction as professed in *The Secret* is a re-statement of this spiritual principle which harnesses the power of our imagination. However, the HUGE failure which *The Secret* so conveniently neglected to state is that you just can't wait for these manifestations to fall from the sky (like they show in the movie). You have to get up off your sofa and put effort, physical and mental motivation behind that imagination process in order for it to become a reality.

There is a very important flip-side to that law - the universe does not differentiate between good, positive, uplifting thoughts vs. bad, negative, destructive thoughts. So whichever of those types of thought forms are in your imagination, they will become reality. I know that this following statement is going to seem harsh, but this law suggests that if your life is surrounded by gloom and negativity, you have put yourself there by your past thoughts and you keep yourself there by your current thoughts and lack of effort to make a change. Allow your imagination to wrap itself around only positive, uplifting thoughts and then just watch and see how fast energy will move into your life to help change your situations.

Our imagination can also lead us into negative situations. It was Eve's imagination that got her into trouble in the Garden of Eden. The serpent did a wonderful job of painting word-pictures within her imagination about the beauty of the fruit and the power which she could behold.

The concept of imagination, also referred to as illusion, is present in the scriptures of the Judean-Christian beliefs, along with several other holy texts of the world, including the Qur'an. All faiths hold some significance to the power of imagination.

A few of the greatest positive examples of the power of imagination in the 20th century were:

> Henry Ford – From his imagination developed the assembly line which revolutionized the automotive and manufacturing industries.

> Walt Disney - From his imagination was born an amazing mouse named Mickey, which has blossomed into a worldwide entertainment empire that brings joy and happiness to millions every year.

> Ray Croc – From his imagination of selling milkshake machines sprang the worldwide empire of McDonald's.

> Oprah Winfrey – From her creative imagination and human compassion developed a worldwide mega-billion dollar media business which brings hope, compassion and empowerment to millions of people each day.

These are just few examples of the tens-of-thousands of imaginative people who impact our lives on a daily basis. Where will your imagination lead you?

There was a movie released in 1984 called *The NeverEnding Story,* which is a wonderful fantasy based on the daydreaming and imagination of a young boy. The movie is a journey through his fears, and examines things like luck and despair while trying to reach the wonderful city of Fantasia. The city of Fantasia is being destroyed by The Nothing, a powerful destructive force. Just like in our lives - if we do nothing, the dreams and goals which blossom from our imagination will die. An interesting note is that this German-made film was the most expensive film project ever produced outside the USA or Russia up to 1984. The powerful message and symbology within this film was well worth its production costs. I highly recommend this movie for parents, teachers and children alike.

Nigel J.T. Thomas, a current modern-day philosopher and Professor at California State University, Los Angeles has this to say about imagination:

"Imagination is what makes our sensory experience meaningful, enabling us to interpret and make sense of it, whether from a conventional perspective or from a fresh, original, individual one. It is what makes perception more than the mere physical stimulation of sense organs. It also produces mental imagery, visual and otherwise, which is what makes it possible for us to think outside the confines of our present perceptual reality, to consider memories of the past and possibilities for the future, and to weigh alternatives against one another. Thus, imagination makes possible all our thinking about what is, what has been, and, perhaps most important, what might be."

From Aristotle back in 300 BC to a modern philosopher like Nigel Thomas in the early 21st Century, one thing still stands true: imagination is a critical component to our human soul and its importance is a key element to branding and defining our character.

L. Frank Baum (1856-1919) was an American author, poet and the creator of *The Wizard of Oz*. His viewpoint on imagination was:

"Imagination has brought mankind through the dark ages to its present state of civilization. Imagination led Columbus to discover America. Imagination led Franklin to electricity. Imagination has given us the steam engine, the telephone, the talking-machine, and the automobile, for these things had to be dreamed of before they became realities. So I believe that dreams – daydreams, you know, with your eyes wide open and your brain machinery whizzing – are likely to lead to the betterment of the world. The imaginative child will become the imaginative man or woman most apt to invent, and therefore to foster civilization."

It is my hope that all parents and teachers develop a healthy positive environment to foster the *phantasia* (fantasy) and *imaginatio* (imagination) within children. Thoughts and imagination play a crucial role in developing ones' overall character. The person branded with an impeccable character, then, is one who is honest, upright and wholesome, not only in their outward life, but also whose quiet meditations and secret imaginations are in harmony with the most pure of positive aspirations.

As suggested by L. Frank Baum, *follow your imagination down the yellow brick road!*

Additional Resources

For information on my Comedy Stage Hypnosis Show, check out www.Hpnotix.com

---

Chapter 5 Scientific Case Study

As I mentioned in the previous chapter, the research here in this chapter also lends scientific support to the message that many motivational speakers, self-help books and sports psychologists have been saying for centuries.

We have heard many times that if we "Imagine doing/having/achieving a goal, that in fact it will happen." Christopher Davoli and Richard Abrams, both psychologists from Washington University, now have some research which backs up the notion that imagination may be more effective in helping us reach our goals than what we had thought. Their experiment had participants imagining certain items while performing various tasks. You can read further about this experiment and the others from the links in the bibliography section.

Davoli's and Abrams' research suggests that the power of imagination is much more than a metaphor, and that it truly does have the capacity to shape our reality.

Chapter 5 Quotes For Thought:

"Imagination will often carry us to worlds that never were. But without it, we go nowhere."
~ Carl Sagan

"Our imagination is the only limit to what we can hope to have in the future." ~ Charles F. Kettering

"Imagination is the beginning of creation. You imagine what you desire, you will what you imagine and at last you create what you will." ~ George Bernard Shaw

"Go confidently in the direction of your dreams. Live the life you have imagined." ~ Henry David Thoreau

"You cannot depend on your eyes when your imagination is out of focus." ~ Mark Twain

"Everything you can imagine is real." ~ Pablo Picasso

"Think left and think right and think low and think high. Oh, the thinks you can think up if only you try!"
~ Dr. Seuss

"It's kind of fun to do the impossible." ~ Walt Disney

Chapter 5 Exercises:

1. What future achievements are still buried deep within your imagination?

2. What goals have you accomplished that you can trace back to your imagination?

3. What can you do to help foster the imagination in your loved ones around you?

Chapter 5 Diary Page:

Chapter 6

Friends Come And Go, But Enemies Accumulate

"When the character of a man is not clear to you, look at his friends." ~ Japanese Proverb

We are judged by the relationships we make and the quality of those people we have in our lives. Therefore, this chapter on relationships is an integral component to our study on character. We will discuss the importance of both *friends* (friends, family, co-workers, etc.) and *enemies*, people we don't like (former-friends, family, co-workers, etc.).

Friends

Friends are choice individuals who are especially drawn to us and us to them – some refer to friends as their 'chosen family' – some feel they are stuck with their biological family, but by choice, choose the friends to become their chosen family. This mutual attraction is based on taste and temperament, with other factors such as affection, sociability, neighborliness, companionship and fellowship. We tend to make friends with those who we have similar interests with (sports, hobbies, careers, volunteering, etc.) and even once in awhile a dose of personal attraction.

A true friend is a rare possession, because they are willing to make sacrifices for one another. A real friend does not ask for explanations of conduct but takes for granted that one is acting from the best of motives. Such confidence conserves and develops ones' worthwhile character.

True friendship is both exclusive and open-hearted. A friend's open-hearted frankness refers to disapproval as well as encouragement, depending on the appropriate situation. A friend will tell you the truth – whether you like it or not! Friends should never flatter. The Book of Proverbs states: "Faithful are the wounds of a friend, but the kisses of an enemy are deceitful." The immortal words of Dr. Seuss address these feelings of true friendship:

"Be who you are and say what you feel, because those who mind don't matter, and those who matter, don't mind."

Former Justice of the United States Supreme Court, Oliver Wendell Holmes once noted that a friend is the only person who has a key to the side door of your heart. "Be very careful," he says, "to whom you trust one of these keys."

A true friend is a constant inspiration, while an evil friend can emotionally drain you like a vampire. Be conscious of those so-called friends who always drain your energy from you – they suck your life-source from you just like a vampire sucking blood. You don't need people like that around you!

One of the most wonderful privileges in life is the ability to weave our hearts together with like-minded souls - our friends. However, if we are to have friends we must show ourselves friendly to others. If there is no sense of a friendly spirit in our hearts, then all other hearts which we come in contact with will seem cold and selfish to us. If you want a friend – you first need to be a friend!

In 350 BC, Aristotle wrote in his *Nicomachean Ethics Book VIII* that friendships can be classified into three categories. Through the ages, even up through today, most philosophers still believe that we can break down our friends into these three groupings:

- Pleasure – What kind of pleasure do you get out of this group of friend? Is it a personal social dynamic, or some other form of pleasure? Friends in this setting may also include sporting, book clubs or needlepoint groups.
- Utility – How useful is this friend to you – and vice versa? Maybe a co-worker or someone with whom you share a car pool. Others in this group would include business associates, coaches and a personal trainer.
- Virtue – What moral or ethical relationship with positive character do we have with this friend? People in this group would be ministers, mentors, teachers, fellow study group members or scout leaders who instill positive qualities within youth.

Does this listing need to be updated? Do you have friends that would not fit into one of these three categories? If so, what would you add? What about our online chat buddies – are they included in one of these three or do they need a new *technology* category of their own?

Many teachers and preachers use a parable like this one to illustrate the importance of friendship:

Two travelers embark together on a journey called life, and after a number of years, come back, where they are asked what kind of world it is. One replies, "It is a cold world. Every person is looking out for themselves, and could care less about people around them. Selfishness was rampant. People closed their hearts against me. I found them suspicious and uncaring. In summary, it is a loveless world." The other traveler said with a smile on his face, "The world is full of friendliness. Wherever I have gone among the poor and among the rich, among the learned and among the uncultured, nothing has surprised me so much as the open acceptance of human hearts. I have found friendship everywhere. Of all the treasures I have gathered on my journey, none are so sweet to me as my friendships."

It was the same world, but the participants were different. Our outlook on life, optimistic or pessimistic, is reflected in the world around us.

As noted in the headline quote to this chapter, a person is no greater than the reflection of their friends. Friends play a large role on our standing in the community, promotions at work and our destiny as a whole. Therefore, let each of us take to heart the importance of our friends, no matter how casual those relationships may be.

There is a great children's fable by Aesop, which talks about the importance of even 'smaller' friendships:

To sum up this fable, a sleeping lion is woken up by a mouse. The lion wants to eat the mouse, but the mouse begs forgiveness and vows to return the favor in the future. Sure enough, hunters trap the lion in a net, but while the hunters are gone to get a cage, the mouse chews the netting and the lion is set free. This story shows no matter how small in stature or frequency, all levels of friendships can be important and meaningful.

Friendship is an innate passion of the human heart; it warms and sweetens and blesses every relationship. A friend in need is a friend indeed. There are many meaningful messages of friendship in the Christian Bible as well as most all other holy texts of world religions. Friendship is touted as the key which unlocks each heart and opens it up to the all-loving heart of the God-force in many religions.

Enemies
Character is formed as much from our enemies as by our friends, and because of that formative influence of our enemies upon our character, we might want to call our enemies 'negative friends'.

An interesting point to discuss here is the fact that Aristotle's three categories of friends which we just reviewed can also be applied to our enemies. There are people whom we keep around us which fall into the 'enemy' category but serve a purpose to us – their purpose is a direct reflection back to pleasure, utility or virtue.

The term 'Frenemy' has been growing in popularity and is a combination of the words friend and enemy. It refers to that person who we feel fits both of those labels. A frenemy is a relationship which is both mutually beneficial or dependent, some might say co-dependent, but is also laced with mistrust and risk. Remember the old saying, "keep your friends close but your enemies closer?" That saying definitely would refer to this group of frenemies. Frenemies have to be watched at all times.

To have enemies we don't necessarily need to be bad or wrong, because all people, businesses, and philosophies in the world have enemies. Good people have enemies. We read many examples of that fact all throughout history and in religious texts.

Enemies can either be real or imagined. A real enemy would be someone whom we know has hurt or harmed us, or who has lost our trust. An imagined enemy is typically a person or group of people who, through propaganda or brainwashing, we have been told to dislike. We see this imagined enemy concept in many radical religions, business and political government scenarios. Also, through our family upbringing we may have been conditioned to believe that an enemy may be someone of a different skin color, nationality or socio-economic class.

It is my thinking that this concept of imagined enemies is based on ignorance, malice and judgment. Education and awareness will overturn this classification of enemy. This is particularly true when it comes to radical political and religious factions. This type of blatant ignorance is what motivates suicide bombers to believe that by killing themselves and those around them, they are doing God's work. Education, awareness, forgiveness and an open, loving heart will diminish the list of imagined enemies – but that takes much time to overturn pre-conditioned prejudices.

The philosophy of *lex talionis* seems to be a natural feeling of the human heart. This philosophy is discussed in the Torah, Quran and the Bible, and is defined as 'an eye for an eye', or in legal terms is known as retributive justice. Early holy texts seem to hold steadfast on this method of justice - i.e., you cut off someone's arm then your arm is cut off.

As societies became more civilized, we see a softening of this type of justice toward enemies. Forgiveness comes into play when Jesus said in (Matt 5:38-39), "You have heard that it was said, "An eye for an eye and a tooth for a tooth". But I say to you, do not resist an evildoer. If anyone strikes you on the right cheek, turn to him the other also."

Forgiveness

When people, products or businesses have done us wrong hate comes easy, but forgiveness is hard. That is probably the biggest lesson to learn here in this chapter. How we deal with our enemies speaks volumes about our character. Forgiveness is the prime lesson in this chapter. We build our character bit by bit, day by day, and we cannot afford to have it eroded by petty spites and revenges. We are not the judges of our enemies, and so everyone who aspires to be a worldly person of character needs to release any judgments and revenges out into the universe.

Robert D. Enright, Professor of Educational Psychology at the University of Wisconsin at Madison and a founding member of the International Forgiveness Institute, says: "To forgive is not to condone, to excuse, to accept, to reconcile and certainly not to forget." Professor Enright also contends: "A person who has been hurt must consciously choose to forgive, a moral choice that is one step along a path that takes time to complete."

Psychologists and social workers tell us that possessing a positive mental health requires letting go of anger. It seems that the most emotionally healthy people are able to 'roll with the punches' and adapt to whatever life events are presented to them. They are also reasonable in their expectations of others – both of their friends and of their enemies.

Forgiveness is the highest form of revenge that a person of character can exhibit. When you unconditionally forgive those who have wronged you, they cannot hurt you anymore because they no longer have any power over you.

We have just spent a few minutes discussing the power of forgiveness as it relates to other people and events in our lives. Now comes the hardest and most important aspect of the forgiveness process – forgiving ourselves! The Toltec Indians believe anything is possible when it comes to dealing from within our inner source. The power is in each of us. The only reason people suffer is because they choose to suffer. Happiness and love are the result of the forgiveness process.

When one hasn't forgiven, then emotions control our behaviors instead of us controlling behaviors. Forgiveness is the only way to heal our inner wounds. The following statement needs to be the healing mantra on your journey of self-forgiveness:

I will no longer beat myself up;
I will no longer be the victim.

Dr. Joyce A. Feldman wrote, "In forgiveness you take back your own power! You fortify yourself. Forgiveness means it's over – really over! You're clear, clean and free!"

As we go through life, we find that it is easier to obey this power of forgiveness than it is to disobey. To obey means a life of blessings and happiness, and growth toward a positive person of character – to disobey means a life of loneliness, struggle and negativity. Love your friends, forgive your enemies and heal yourself!

Chapter 6 Scientific Case Studies

(1) A recent study at the University of Exeter in the United Kingdom examines the importance of friendship in athletics.

The study shows that the social support of friends plays a significant role when an athlete is under stress. The research was done on amateur golfers all under stress. It found that those golfers who had a large social support group could improve their scores by one shot per round of golf. And on the contrary, those with the lowest level of support could see a decrease of up to three shots per round.

"Our study reveals the ongoing support of friends and family to be one of the most important factors influencing sports performance. While training, tactics, and luck all play a part, the encouraging words or kind gestures of a partner or friend can make the difference between a footballer scoring that winning goal, or a sprinter achieving a record time. The encouragement and support of friends and family clearly plays a massive part in building confidence, which is so important when the pressure is on," stated Dr. Tim Rees from the University of Exeter's School of Sport and Health Sciences.

I am sure this will just be the start of research on the significance of friendships. If this level of positive result is evident in golf, just think of the positive effects of friends in other sports, the workplace, and maybe even for students in school.

(2) Sociologist Gerald Mollenhorst from the Netherlands is involved in a social network study.

Mollenhorst's study is interested in questions like: Who do you talk with regarding important personal issues? Who helps you with home projects? Who do you pop by to see? Where did you get to know that person? Where do you meet that person now? The studies are exploring the dynamics of choice and individualism as it relates to friendships. One of his very interesting conclusions thus far is: you lose about half of your close network members (friends) every seven years.

That is great information to have because as we all grow and develop into different areas in our lives, it is perfectly normal to develop new friendships along the way.

Chapter 6 Quotes For Thought:

"We read that we ought to forgive our enemies, but we do not read that we ought to forgive our friends."
~ Francis Bacon

"Be generous and understanding. Let no one come to you without feeling better and happier when they leave. Be the living expression of God's kindness: with kindness on your face.... in your eyes... in your smile... in your warm greeting." ~ Mother Teresa

"Am I not destroying my enemies when I make friends of them?" ~ Abraham Lincoln

"It is easy to be nice, even to an enemy - from lack of character." ~ Dag Hammarskjold

"Listen to your enemy, for God is talking."
~ Jewish Proverb

"Forgive your enemies, but never forget their names."
~ John F. Kennedy

"Wishing to be friends is quick work, but friendship is a slow ripening fruit." ~ Aristotle

"Love is the only force capable of transforming an enemy into friend." ~ Martin Luther King, Jr.

Chapter 6 Exercises:

1. How have friends and enemies had a positive and/or negative effect on circumstances in your life?

2. Are there friends that you have not seen in awhile? Are there any that you have a yearning to reconnect with?

3. How has the act of forgiveness been beneficial in your life? Are there some people that you need to forgive today?

4. What emotions do you need to forgive yourself on so that you can take your life to the next level?

Chapter 6 Diary Page:

Chapter 7

Nothing Will Work Unless You Do

> *"I've always believed that if you put in the work, the results will come."* ~ Michael Jordan

Labor is a duty and an untold blessing to the human race. Humans are responsible for achieving their destiny through their works and deeds. In order to accomplish that task, we must labor on our goals. Those physical activities which we place into motion are our duty and a blessing, but to some, may also feel like a burden. This chapter will use the words work, labor and effort synonymously to refer to the action behind a given task.

We have previously discussed the act of exuding effort behind our purpose and in all that we do in life. As this chapter's title states, which are words by Ms. Maya Angelou, nothing will be accomplished in your life or in society without work behind it. Work is an integral component to defining who you are and defining your character.

In the chapter on *Purpose*, we learned the difference between negative purpose careers versus positive purpose careers. This chapter on *Work* is going to focus on positive character building, life-affirming, positive purpose careers. When you really think

107

about it, work is the underlying force which allows your individuality to stand in the forefront, have your imagination become reality, define who you are from your purpose, maintain healthy relationships and keep you on a faithful path.

Labor is honorable. To do common work uncommonly well is the essence of a successful person with character. There is a painting in the Louvre Museum in Paris by Seville, Spain painter Murillo (Angel's Kitchen 1646), which depicts the interior of a Franciscan Monastery Kitchen. However, it is not the mortal clergy doing the work in the kitchen; it is several beautiful white-winged angels. One angel serenely places a kettle on the fire to boil, another is lifting up a pail of water with heavenly grace, and one is at the side-board reaching for plates. All are so busy and working with such a will and grace that somehow you forget their physical surroundings. You think only of the angels, and how very natural and beautiful kitchen work is - just what angels would do, should it be required of them. That painting is an analogy of how we should treat our earthly work; we need to do our common work with the grace and will of an angel.

The *spirit* toward your work is a major factor in the successful completion of any task. Pity goes out to the person who does not find enjoyment in their daily occupation. Unhappy workers are like trying to put a square peg into a round hole. No person can do their very best work under such uncomfortable conditions. One needs to turn their avocation into their vocation. Turn what you *love* doing into what you *have* to do!

Intelligent work in an honorable occupation is a blessing. Labor will enlarge your capacity for work. Meaning, the more well-directed labor we perform, the more we are able to accomplish. There is truth to the old saying, "If you want something done, give it to the busiest person." Work is necessary for your healthy peace of mind as well as for a healthy physical body. A day of worry is more exhausting than a week of work. With today's current economic situation and the high rate of unemployment, most of us can relate to that statement when we were unemployed and dealing with the job search and harassing bill collectors. Worry upsets our whole system, while work keeps our system in health and good working order. Exercise of the muscles keeps the body in good health, while exercise of the brain brings peace of mind.

A good precaution toward work is to never hurry. Mother Nature never does. For example, think of the gradual growth of a mighty oak tree or the years of decay by a flowing river to create the beauty of a gorge. The first bit of advice a Park Ranger gives a young explorer before descending the narrow path down to the base of the Grand Canyon is, "Go slowly and steadily, not trying to walk too fast or loitering in one place. By all means pause now and then." A great secret to progress in life is never hurry and never loiter. Remember the fable of the tortoise and the hare? "Haste," says an ancient Palestinian Proverb, "cometh of the evil one, but patience openeth the Gates of Felicity." Many people seem to feel that they can save time by hurrying. That philosophy is a big mistake. It is much more important to do a task well than to get through it quickly. Hurriedness not only spoils work, but life too. It is splendid to work hard, but it is unwise to hurry or to be anxious.

Diligence in your work brings its own reward, and sometimes your success may even come by accident. Remember that Columbus discovered America while actually searching for a western passage to India. Many of the most successful people owe their success to vigor rather than to cleverness. Let two people start in life: one with brilliant abilities, but careless and self-indulgent; the other comparatively slow, but industrious, careful and highly-principled - and the latter over time will out-distance the more brilliant competitor. No advantage in life, no cleverness, no rich friends or powerful relations will make up for the zeal and vigor in a person with character.

Now comes the task of choosing what you want to do for your life's work. We ask children when they are very young, "what do you want to be when you grow up?" Their answers at that age will usually have no reflection on what they will actually be doing as adults. Everyone's dreams and desires differ in that area:

Little Jimmy and Jean are neighbors and were playing together in the backyard. "Don't you wish you were a bird, Jimmy, and could fly up in the sky?"

asked little Jean. "No," said Jimmy sternly. "I'd rather be an elephant and squirt water through my nose."

Many people have difficulty trying to decipher the obscure variety of things they want to become, and that is compounded by the ever-increasing choices of occupations. People can become very puzzled as to how to go about choosing their life's work. Each person has their various desires and aptitudes. Whatever you desire to become – a computer programmer, news reporter, mechanic, engineer, business owner, doctor, lawyer, author, painter, teacher or preacher – make an in-depth study of that occupation, its advantages and disadvantages as they pertain to your beliefs as to what you can do and become. Do this with each occupation which appeals to your curiosity. Read, think and ask questions of people currently in that profession. Your vocation needs to be the one that intersects your aptitude and ability at the point of your creative desires. And most importantly, don't worry too much about making mistakes; you can always change professions as you mature and become more educated. According to the Bureau of Labor Statistics for the United States, the average person will only stay at one job for 4.1 years. Therefore, an average person will have 7-10 different jobs within their lifetime.

Personal happiness needs to be your motivating force for choosing a vocation. Too many parents try to pressure their children into choosing a profession based on *their* wants and unfulfilled goals. When this happens, the children become unhappy adults in miserable occupations that they feel don't fit them. Remember the chapter on *Individuality* – stand up for your wants and feelings. Live for yourself and your personal happiness – not for your parents!

These following three steps are designed to help you define an occupational match OR help you redefine *yourself* if you are thinking of making a career change OR if you are thinking of launching a new product or service within your business. This exercise should be done every few years to make sure that your professional career identity is staying current with the changing times and your changing clientele.

1. Continually re-assess your interests. Look for those items that you do best, those things that come easiest for you, those tasks you seem to be doing most frequently, and those things you get the most satisfaction from doing. Ask yourself, "What are my interests and experiences?"

2. Know the market. Do your homework - research to find out who needs your skills, services or products. Identify and understand their concerns. Your market base is not limited to your current client base; think globally and don't forget to include colleagues, family, friends, other businesses, and even your competitors as your global market base. This point can change frequently with our fast-paced global

economy. You need to re-assess this point and keep up or you will get left along the wayside. Cutting-edge ideas and plans will keep you or your company fresh, and a leading source within your niche.

3. Create a mission statement. A mission statement is not only for Fortune 500 companies - it is a useful tool for every individual and business, no matter the size. A mission statement defines your purpose and goals. There are many free examples of mission statements available on the Internet. Here are four sub-points to keep in mind as you develop a mission statement of your own:

- Identify your short-term and long-term goals
- Describe your ideal customer or ideal working situation
- Focus on clarity and simplicity
- Seek feedback

Your mission statement is only useful if it can be understood by those who read it and will be financially rewarding if you follow what you have written - in other words, practice what you preach!

When we become working adults, there is a different shift on identity issues which come into play. These are important items to discuss as they pertain to developing personal character.

Who are you?
What do you do?

Those are probably the two most asked questions at business networking events. We have all been to cocktail parties, networking events or chatting online when we are asked one or both of those questions. It is vitally important for the benefit of our self-esteem and self-identity that we separate those two questions. We ARE NOT what we do! We are (at least when you are done reading this book), wonderful, loving, caring, thoughtful, giving, helpful, smart, intelligent, human beings of character that make a difference in the world! What you do is your career, occupation or profession.

Too many people identify themselves by their occupation and not by who they are - an individual with unique and loving qualities. Make sure that your personal identity is separate from your business and vocational identity. The above exercise will help you set personal and/or professional boundaries. Remember, you are *who you are*, you are not *what you do*!

Comedian George Carlin was making fun of work in one of his routines. He said, "Most people work just hard enough not to get fired and get paid just enough money not to quit." Although he was making a joke, that statement is pretty much a fact. Unfortunately it is the work-ethic motto for many individuals, especially here in the United States. Laziness and a sense of entitlement has fostered this mentality. We did not see that laziness motto in our grandparents or great-grandparents who worked hard to develop a better life for their family. We also do not see that work ethic in people immigrating to the United States – they work circles around the rest.

I feel there are two issues which have helped to perpetuate the laziness and sense of entitlement philosophy in the United States. One is the over-protection of labor unions and the other is the concept of tenure.

Too many individuals are protected by their labor unions who should have been fired years ago. Low productivity, drug abuse and constant tardiness should not be allowed in any workplace environment. Unions need to stop enabling poor workers and start looking at the larger issues facing the economy and global workplace. I will admit that unions have played an important part in prior history to protect workers from unethical and unsafe conditions within a company. However, if both a company and its workers had high ethical standards and followed the principles within this book, then labor unions would no longer be needed.

The concept of tenure has kept people in jobs who should be long gone, especially in education. Tenure means that someone is entitled to keep their position just because they have been at it for a certain length of time. People get stale and lose interest over time and they should not be protected in that position. There are many problems in the U.S. educational system which are due to tenure.

Your sense of ethics, character and motivation; coupled with a track record of personal productivity should be the reasons you keep a job, not due to a union or tenure. All employees need to be held accountable for their actions. Their advancement in salary and status needs to be based on merit and performance, not just by time. This also holds true for a company. The marketplace will determine a company's success or failure based on its fulfillment of customer needs. A recent example of this was the failing U.S. automakers who are being over-taken by more innovative and customer-focused vehicles being supplied by foreign automakers.

Your work is a defining element of your character. Not only in *what* you do, but also in *how* you do it. All positive purpose occupations work together in one cohesive manner for the betterment of society. Choose a career path that will motivate you to get up every morning and face a new and exciting day. Embrace your labor because it gives you the chance to love and to work and to play, and to be satisfied with a happy heart, knowing you are doing your best.

Chapter 7 Scientific Case Studies

Happy at work equates to happy at home. A recent study at Kansas State University shows that invigorated and dedicated employees take those positive qualities home for a happier home life.

"Our research indicated that individuals who were engaged in positive experiences at work and who shared those experiences with significant others perceived themselves as better able to deal with issues at home, became better companions and became more effective overall in the home environment. Our results indicate that engagement is controlled by situational factors that are manageable by the organization," stated Professor Satoris Culbertson.

Choosing a happy vocation as discussed in this chapter is only part of the work experience. You also have to have workplace surroundings that foster a positive work experience. As this study detailed, organizations can play a crucial part in developing more positive workplace experiences which carry over into home life as well. Things such as positive reinforcement vs. negative reinforcement, and allowing for a balance of work / home time are all part of this equation. Happily engaged workers have fewer health issues, less time off, are more productive, and tend to stay longer with an employer. All of those items can increase the profitability of any company.

Chapter 7 Quotes For Thought:

"Your work is to discover your world and then with all your heart give yourself to it." ~ Buddha

"The miracle is not that we do this work, but that we are happy to do it." ~ Mother Teresa

"Success in its highest and noblest form calls for peace of mind and enjoyment and happiness which come only to the man who has found the work that he likes best." ~ Napoleon Hill

"A lot of people quit looking for work as soon as they find a job." ~ Zig Ziglar

"The only place success comes before work is in the dictionary." ~ Vince Lombardi

"It took a lot of blood, sweat and tears to get to where we are today, but we have just begun. Today we begin in earnest the work of making sure that the world we leave our children is just a little bit better than the one we inhabit today." ~ Barack Obama

"Whatever your life's work is, do it well. A man should do his job so well that the living, the dead, and the unborn could do it no better." ~ Martin Luther King, Jr.

118

Chapter 7 Exercises:

1. Describe your perfect occupation. Are you doing it? If not, what can you do to move into that perfect career?

2. List a few of the qualities that you associate with your optimum career of character.

3. What is your answer to the questions: What do you do? Who are you? Tell me about yourself.

Chapter 7 Diary Page:

Chapter 8

The Element of Faith

> *"I do not pray for success, I ask for faithfulness."*
> ~ Mother Teresa

Faith in oneself is essential to building good character. The type of faith being referred to here is not one of a nebulous religious context but more of a hardcore trust, confidence and dependence on a powerful sense of inner knowing. This form of self-reliance is a guiding force of character. It enables a person to be evenly balanced in all aspects of life.

Faith in oneself is a skill needed in all forms of achievement. The person who has lost their inner faith is more than half defeated before they even begin. Leadership requires self-confidence - leadership of yourself and leadership of those around you.

Faith is a key component to all aspects of knowledge, whether it be science, history or philosophy. Religion does not have an exclusive ownership on faith - however, religious factions seem to be the ones who exploit faith the most. We must have confidence in the awareness of our senses and trustworthiness in our observations, deductions and conclusions. We must have faith in the observations and testimony of others - otherwise there would be no such thing as history or science. As William Wordsworth said, "Faith is a passionate intuition." Follow that inner intuition in all aspects of your life.

Trust is that force on which business, governments and the banking systems operate. On every piece of currency printed in the United States is the slogan 'In God We Trust'. We trust that the piece of currency will still hold enough value to purchase the product or service which we require – this holds true in all other countries as well. The commercial credit and banking system runs on trust; however, with the recent economic crashes in the past couple years, many people all over the world have lost faith in those banking and currency markets.

Without faith there would be no social or community life, no homes, no government and no civilization. There also must be a reasonable level of confidence among other people in order for a society to be safe, wholesome and prosperous. Just think how many automobile accidents would occur each day if we did not have the faith in other drivers that they will obey the street signs. When faith falters in a society, panic and disorder ensues. We see this in many neighborhoods where drugs, crime and gang activity is rampant.

Another important factor in the formation of good character is having faith in fellow-mankind. Having confidence in others helps them to be at their best, and is an integral component to developing those friendships which we just discussed in a previous chapter. In spite of seemingly ongoing disappointments, it still remains true that we should continue to have faith in people, and motivate our friends to try again and to do better.

Parents and teachers must show an abundance of faith in their children and students. Nothing will inspire them more as far as human influence is concerned than the consciousness of your faith in them. Here is an empowering mantra for teachers to use in the classroom:

I have faith to believe that there are future noted leaders here in my classroom. I have confidence in your abilities as bright and successful men and women.

We all need more of that optimistic faith in our fellow human beings. Such faith is worthwhile, both in the fact that it is good for those who are trusted, and reciprocally it is good for those who trust. Showing that level of faith in others is a Godlike quality and is worthy of daily emulation among all of us.

Doubt and faith are on opposite ends of the spectrum. Doubt is the darkness and negative end filled with turmoil and thunderous storms, as described in some writings. Faith is the bright and positive end of that spectrum, filled with clear skies, and peaceful tranquil waters. All through our lives and even within differing events, we move along that continuum. A person living a life of character is one who can stay closer toward the end of faith.

It's a sliding scale of life's events, but knowing that goodness, peace and love awaits us at the end of faith is a motivating factor to keep us away from doubt.

Doubt  *Faith*

Faith and the power of faith have been recognized for centuries in the teachings and preaching of numerous theologians and philosophers. I am not promoting one religious belief over the other, because in my opinion, all of the world's religions have a place and a meaning. With that said, one of my favorite quotes regarding the broader spirituality of faith comes from the 20th century Christian mystic philosopher and former French schoolteacher, Simone Weil. She stated: "The hunger of the soul is not a belief, it is a certainty." That 'certainty of the soul's hunger' of which she speaks is that of faith – a kind of faith that nurtures and sustains all of us.

In his book *Raw Faith*, best-selling author John Kirvan begins to enlighten us on this sense of 'certainty' that Simone Weil professed. John suggests that:

"Faith is not a simple profession of what you accept as true . . . not something stirred up in the moments of grandeur or terror . . . not a spiritual grace note to an ordinary life . . . not spiritual brand loyalty. Faith is something else again. It is another way of knowing what is most familiar to us and at the same time coming to know a world beyond the familiar, beyond everything that can be reached by our mind

124

and senses. It is what you do, how you respond in the face of the unfathomable mystery that lies at the core of everything we are, of everything we experience. Faith is our submission to, our embrace of, the unknowable as the cornerstone of our lives."

There is a wonderful story, or parable if you will, that teaches us this embrace of certainty or embrace of faith:

Two traveling angels stopped to spend the night in the home of a wealthy family. The family was rude and refused to let the angels stay in the mansion's guest room. Instead the angels were given a small space in the cold basement. As they made their bed on the hard floor, the older angel saw a hole in the wall and repaired it.

When the younger angel asked why, the older angel replied, "Things aren't always what they seem."

The next night the pair of angels came to rest at the house of a very poor, but very hospitable farmer and his wife. After sharing what little food they had, the couple let the angels sleep in their bed where they could have a good night's rest.

When the sun came up the next morning the angels found the farmer and his wife in tears. Their only cow, whose milk had been their sole income, lay dead in the field.

The younger angel was infuriated and asked the older angel how he could have let this happen? The first man had everything yet you helped him, he accused. The second family had little but was willing to share everything, and you let the cow die.

"Things aren't always what they seem," the older angel replied.

"When we stayed in the basement of the mansion, I noticed there was gold stored in that hole in the wall. Since the owner was obsessed with greed and unwilling to share his good fortune, I sealed the wall so he wouldn't find it."

"Then, last night as we slept in the farmer's bed, the angel of death came for his wife. I gave him the cow instead. Things aren't always what they seem."

Sometimes that is exactly what happens when things don't turn out the way we feel they should. If you have faith, you just need to trust that every outcome is always to your advantage, whether or not you believe it at the time. It is that same power of certainty that Simone Weil discussed.

How many of you reading this book here today would have to honestly answer that you feel more like the younger angel than the older angel? As we grow and develop into empowered individuals of character it will be our trust in that certainty - or if you will, our *faith* in faith - which will allow us to remain steadfast on our journey through life.

As we look back over this day, the past week, the past month, the past years, and take time to reflect on the things that we did and did not do – all of the wondrous things and all of the sorrows that have beseeched our lives - there might be several of us who might be asking, "where was God in our lives at some of those particular moments?" or "why did we have to go through that experience?" If one has that depth of certainty (faith) that Simone Weil and John Kirvan mention, then one would not need to be asking these questions.

I will be the first one to admit that the depth of faith which Simone and John describe is much harder to place into action than it is to write about. What we need to remember, and take to heart in any and all situations, are the words of the older angel: "things aren't always as they seem." It is easy to reassure ourselves once we have all the facts or are able to see the situation from a different perspective. The certainty of knowing that both Simone Weil and John Kirvan are professing tells us that we do not need to know or see everything. *Raw Faith* is that deep-seated inner knowing of the unfathomable mysteries. As John so wisely puts it: "Faith is our submission to, our embrace of, the unknowable as the cornerstone of our lives."

The second part of that statement – "the cornerstone of our lives" - is equally important to the faith factor for character. Once we have that depth of faith, we need to live it every day in every way. We all had it at one time when we were children, but as we have grown older, that depth of faith for which is spoken seems to elude many. Here is an example of what I mean:

In 1904, when Peter Pan began playing in London, children were enthralled by the flying hero of Never-Never Land. So thrilled, in fact, that they wanted to be just like him: "If you only believe, you can fly!"

When J. M. Barrie, the writer of Peter Pan, began hearing from distraught parents whose children had injured themselves by attempting to fly, he changed the script so that Tinkerbelle's fairy dust was needed in order to fly.

That is the power of certainty – that is the power of faith. We all need to return to that child-like openness and acceptance, and build our lives on a solid foundation.

Laying the foundation of character in our life must include a cornerstone of FAITH!

Chapter 8 Scientific Case Study

A recent study from the University of British Columbia in Canada suggests that spirituality, and not religious practices, determine how happy children are.

Dr. Mark Holder and his colleagues found that children who said they were more spiritual were happier. Previous studies have shown that spirituality and religiousness have increased effects on adults and adolescents, but this study with children shows that spirituality is the key to childhood happiness. Religious practices had no significant value of importance in the children.

According to this group of researchers, "enhancing personal meaning may be a key factor in the relation between spirituality and happiness." They suggest that strategies aimed at increasing personal meaning in children - such as expressing kindness towards others and recording these acts of kindness, as well as acts of altruism and volunteering - may help to make children happier.

The traits of spirituality that were examined in this study parallel those we have been discussing in this chapter on faith. It gets back to my initial comment that parents, preachers, and teachers must help empower children with a positive sense of faith. Just imagine the benefits future generations will see if we can start developing faithful character in all children at an early age.

Chapter 8 Quotes For Thought:

"He who has faith has... an inward reservoir of courage, hope, confidence, calmness, and assuring trust that all will come out well - even though to the world it may appear to come out most badly." ~ B.C. Forbes

"Faith... must be enforced by reason.... When faith becomes blind it dies." ~ Gandhi

"In faith there is enough light for those who want to believe and enough shadows to blind those who don't." ~ Blaise Pascal

"A little faith will bring your soul to heaven, but a lot of faith will bring heaven to your soul." ~ Unknown

"Faith is taking the first step even when you don't see the whole staircase." ~ Martin Luther King, Jr.

"Feed your faith and your fears will starve to death." ~ Unknown

"A man of courage is also full of faith." ~ Cicero

"Be faithful in small things because it is in them that your strength lies." ~ Mother Teresa

Chapter 8 Questions:

1. What is your definition of faith?

2. Describe an incident in your life when faith got you through a rough time.

3. List a few qualities that you associate with faith.

4. How can you help to instill some of those qualities of faith in others within your family or neighborhood?

5. What do you need to do in order to strengthen a deeper conviction of faith within yourself?

Chapter 8 Diary Page:

Chapter 9

Character Is A Victory, Not A Gift

> *"A man who stands for nothing will fall for anything."*
> ~ Malcolm X

Character is not made up of mere fragments or component parts, some of which have been discussed in the preceding chapters. Character is the sum of ALL component parts blended into a whole. Character, like a product's brand, is an entity, the sum-total of the expression of what is reflected in one's personality. The exploration of the elements of character discussed on these pages was not intended to be complete, but rather a glimpse into the many-sidedness of human character.

I think that the following story speaks volumes to the elements we have been discussing:

A millionaire once gave a contractor an order to build a house. He left most of the decisions up to the contractor. The contractor was permitted to select the plan, choose the materials, and supervise every phase of the construction process. He thought that here was an opportunity for him to make some extra money, so he used the poorest materials and shoddiest of workmanship. When the house was finished and the contractor went to the millionaire to notify him of that fact, it was much to his surprise when he was told: "This house is for you and your family, and you may live in it as long as you please. It is yours forever." Too late for the contractor; instead of cheating his employer, he had been cheating himself. More than that, he was to have before him for the rest of his days a perpetual reminder of his ruthless lack of character.

When we fail to use the materials that the Universe has placed before us to build a strong, true and noble positive character, we are cheating no one as badly as we are cheating ourselves. Other people have to live with us part of the time, but we have to live with ourselves all the time - and we shall come to regret the results of our foolish or careless building far more than the contractor came to regret the inferior house which he built.

One of the reasons why some people do not rise to their full potential is because they have fears – fear of success and fear of failure. Nelson Mandela addressed those fears in his 1994 Inaugural Speech:

"Our deepest fear is not that we are inadequate. Our deepest fear is that we are powerful beyond measure. It is our light, not our darkness, that frightens us most. We ask ourselves, who am I to be brilliant, gorgeous, talented and fabulous? Actually, who are you not to be? You are a child of God. Your playing small doesn't serve this world. There's nothing enlightened about shrinking so that other people won't feel insecure around you. We were born to manifest the glory of God that is within us.

134

It is not just in some of us - it's in everyone. And as we let our own light shine, we unconsciously give other people permission to do the same. And as we are liberated from our own fear, our presence automatically liberates others."

"Men often become what they believe themselves to be. If I believe I cannot do something, it makes me incapable of doing it. But when I believe I can, then I acquire the ability to do it even if I didn't have it in the beginning," says Gandhi. Don't limit the growth of your character by fears. Ralph Waldo Emerson reminds us: "What lies behind us and what lies before us are tiny matters compared to what lies within us." There is greatness within you. Develop your character's brand so you will be an extraordinary person!

"We must overcome the notion that we must be regular; it robs us of the chance to be extraordinary and leads us to the mediocre." Those are the words spoken by renowned actress, teacher and author, Uta Hagen. Although those words were meant for her acting students, like Jack Lemon, it is a strong principle to incorporate into our character's brand. Always be and do your best! Why wallow in a pit of mediocrity when you have the abilities to soar to new heights of excellence?

Winston Churchill's first speech to the House of Commons three days after becoming Britain's Prime Minister, at the beginning of World War II, went like this:

135

"I have nothing to offer but blood, toil, tears and sweat. We have before us an ordeal of the most grievous kind. We have before us many, many long months of struggle and of suffering. You ask, what is our policy? I can say: It is to wage war, by sea, land, and air, with all our might and with all the strength that God can give us; to wage war against a monstrous tyranny, never surpassed in the dark. That is our policy. You ask, what is our aim? I can answer in one word: It is victory, victory at all costs, victory in spite of all terror, victory, however long and hard the road may be; for without victory, there is no survival."

Although Uta Hagen's and Winston Churchill's comments are quite different, the underlying message is the same: excellence, not mediocrity leads to victory. The words here in this chapter by Mr. Churchill, "...to wage war against a monstrous tyranny, never surpassed in the dark," also reflect back to the movie *The NeverEnding Story* discussed in Chapter 5. Despair and doing nothing is a dark inner tyranny which we each have to overcome on our path to achieving character.

I know I have been hard on parents and teachers in this book; however, those two groups need to realize the supreme importance which they play on building the foundation in the lives of children. We need to educate and instill these values, starting today, in children. This world is a mess from unscrupulous individuals across all professions, and it will be today's children who will mature to become tomorrow's leaders. Those leaders will have many issues to confront and they need to be equipped with a strong sense of self and positive character in order to move society ahead.

While talking with Jennifer about writing the foreword for this book, she reminded me of one theme which is present in most therapy cases – the old saying, "an apple doesn't fall far from the tree," sums up that theme. In other words, the psychological disorders found in many individuals have a direct correlation back to the psychosis and conditioning from their parents. The future well-being of our children relies on the awareness of the parents and those other individuals who directly influence them. This goes back to taking responsibility and recognizing the role you play in a child's life. Again, the mental health and success of tomorrow's generation rests firmly on the shoulders of today's parents.

We now come full circle from the statement I made in the *Preface* section - parents must play a crucial role in equipping and branding their children with these elements of character. I hope parents now see the importance of that statement and will join me in supporting this cause of character development. Character development begins at home. Positive education begins at home. Children need to look at home for their role models.

In some educational settings, a teacher spends more hours per day with a child than a parent. That is the reason I have been so forceful on teachers in this book. Be a teacher or school district leader because you want to inspire the hearts and minds of future leaders, not just because you need to collect a paycheck. Realize the importance of your *role model* position in the lives of kids.

It is refreshing to see that a current role model for personal excellence comes from R&B singing sensation Rihanna. Recently, Rihanna had her personal motto tattooed backwards near her right shoulder so that she can read it every time she looks in a mirror:

"*Never a failure, always a lesson*"

These are words that we all could adapt as our personal motto. It teaches us to look at things as lessons in life instead of mistakes. What personal motto would you write for yourself?

We have spent several chapters of this book examining what some might say are six unrelated topics – individuality, purpose, imagination, friends, work and faith. However, when we place them under this context of character, we see how their importance transcends each other and blends together to produce a powerful force which will uplift each of us into a self-determined person having a life filled with positive character.

Abraham Lincoln once said, "Character is like a tree and reputation like its shadow. The shadow is what we think of it; the tree is the real thing." Your character is your brand of the real thing!

What brand identity and legacy are you going to leave behind for future generations? By adhering to the concepts presented in this book, you will have a powerful legacy of service, love, charity and achievement. Do not rob yourself of those accomplishments by not developing a positive character brand image.

The musical group Trans-Siberian Orchestra has a beautiful, what I refer to as a 'rock-opera' performance called *Beethoven's Last Night*. It is a powerful and moving show which takes place in 1827 and looks at the last night in the life of composer Ludwig von Beethoven. One song in particular, sums up all that we have been discussing here – *What Is Eternal* (words and music by Paul O'Neill and Robert Kinkel).

> "...And who would have thought
> That my fate it would conjure
> This twist in the road
> On which I have wandered
>
> Each vision and dream now
> Completely dismembered
> To give one's whole life
> And find nothing's
> Remembered
>
> And what good is a life
> That leaves nothing behind
> Not a thought or a dream
> That might echo in time

The years and the hours
The seconds and minutes
And everything that
My life has placed in it
BETRAYED..."

Don't wait until the final hours of your life to ask these same questions that Beethoven does in this song!

Don't wait until it is too late to wonder what you will be remembered for!

Don't let the weight of your fears cost you anymore of your unexplored dreams!

Don't waste precious time on things that have no purpose!

Don't betray yourself by not becoming all that you can be!

What is eternal? *You* are eternal! Your deeds in a character filled life are eternal! Vow to yourself here and now that you will brand yourself as a person of character. Let your achievements echo throughout time to shine upon you and future generations by harnessing the combined power of the six elements which we discussed:

Stand out as a powerful individual!

Follow your true purpose!

Let your imagination soar!

Hold your friends near and dear!

Work and labor with zeal and vigor!

Live by faith!

Branding your character will allow you to live a dynamic life – it's your destiny!

> "Watch your thoughts, they become words;
> Watch your words, they become actions;
> Watch your actions, they become habits;
> Watch your habits, they become character;
> Watch your character, for it becomes your destiny."
> ~ Unknown

Chapter 9 Diary Page:

Character In Action - Tokyo

Trust and honesty were, at one time, mainstay ideals in American culture. Most of us remember stories from our parents, grandparents and great-grandparents about times when they would leave their home and not even lock the doors. We have seen TV programs and heard relatives talk about times when shoplifting and stealing were virtually non-existent. Some of these ideals of trust and honesty are still prevalent in small-town rural America, but in the large metropolitan areas it is shameful that they are long gone.

CBS News Sunday Morning did a story on trust in a large city of 12 million people. Trust is such an ingrained cultural norm that there are even vending machines on the streets that sell beer and whiskey, and underage kids mostly don't buy. These kids have a trust instilled into them on following the honor system. This wonderful ideal of trust is the societal norm in Tokyo and throughout Japan. In fact, Japan's current day values remind us of how America once was. When you live in this type of culture where trust is the norm, there is a peace of mind and a degree of security that emanates throughout the people. Everyone is looking out for each other, both on the individual level and on the societal level. You do good for someone else because you know when the time comes and you are in need, someone will do good for you.

Most kids today learn the saying, 'finder's keepers, and loser's weepers'. This is not how it is in Japan or how it once was in America, nor how it should be anywhere!

CBS News reported: "Over 300,000 umbrellas are turned into Tokyo's central lost and found warehouse each year. In fact, last year, wallets and purses that contained $24 million were turned into the lost and found, and much of that money made it back to their owner's pocket."   In fact, on many occasions, a person who finds a lost wallet or purse will go out of their way to personally return it to the rightful owner.

This example of character in action is a model that should be implemented throughout the world.

Character In Action – ABC's Extreme Makeover: Home Edition

The current fad on US television is that of reality shows. One current show which has an amazing impact on peoples' lives and exemplifies the qualities we have been discussing in this book is *ABC's Extreme Makeover: Home Edition*. It's a reality show with social merit. People in need write to the producers and ask for help to remodel or build them a new house.

A local homebuilder donates and coordinates all the carpenters, plumbers, electricians, roofers, painters and other skilled trades necessary to build a house in one week. This show has the power to mobilize an entire community to donate their time and resources to help a neighboring family.

All products and services on the weekly show are donated by the various companies to build and decorate an entire house. All the lumber, landscape, heating and ventilation – everything down to a single nail has been donated by companies with a social conscience. The major sponsors for every show include ABC TV, Sears, Disney, CVS Pharmacy, Southwest Airlines, and Ford Motor Company.

It is heart-warming to watch this show and see how a community will rally behind one of their own. Typically the new house is built for a police, fire, military, or underprivileged family. Many times the show will also help out with a community center, school, non-profit organization; in one case they even built a new Veteran's Center on the Navajo Reservation dedicated to Navajo Military Service Personnel.

The show's host Ty Pennington said, "Great things can happen when you work together." That seems to be the theme of this show and is a great theme for everyone to adapt. The cast, crew, and volunteers at every home-build bring hope to a deserving family. Hope is a powerful healing tool – to heal a family, a neighborhood, and an entire community.

How can you work together and bring hope to those around you?

Character In Action – Liza

Throughout the years, it was entertainment etiquette here in Las Vegas that when stars came to perform, they would do a special free private concert for the rest of the Las Vegas entertainment community. Those shows were usually around 2am, which insured all the other performers would be done with their shows and could make it to that private event. Many visiting entertainers would use this special show as an opportunity to try out new songs, new choreography and new jokes. Liza Minnelli is the only performer who still does this for the rest of the entertainment community. I have had the privilege to see two of her private shows.

It is so nice to see that at least one living-legend superstar still has the heart, love, commitment and character to give back to the fellow entertainment community. Liza is one classy lady!

When Liza performed in Primm, NV, which is about 35 miles south of Las Vegas, a couple of friends and I were her guests for the evening. As most know, she has been in the news media quite a bit over the years for many issues, including her health, but I have to tell you, she is amazing on stage and can still sing and dance with the best of them. She commented on how she recently lost 44 pounds (she looked great), and has had two hip replacements which have not slowed her down from dancing all over the stage. The concert was scheduled to run 90 minutes; however, she was having such a great time and the audience gave her several standing ovations, so she kept singing - the concert was just a few minutes shy of two hours!

After meeting everyone with backstage passes, she asked a few of us to join her for a private dinner at a restaurant in the resort. The restaurant had a private section roped-off in the back just for her party. Three very large security guards were standing along the rope to make sure our dinner was uninterrupted from cameras and autograph seekers. The security was so tight that even one of her dancers who forgot his backstage pass was not able to enter until she waved him in. Liza was so gracious and everyone was enjoying an evening of chatting and laughter - and guess what, she picked up the tab for all of us!

This personal story is a reminder that things are not always as they seem. No matter what we may read or see in the media, those sensationalized stories typically do not represent the true character of an individual. It was truly an honor and privilege to meet Liza. Not many people can say that they have had dinner with Liza Minnelli!

148

Bibliography

Amezquith, Hector. *Thought, The Greatest Power Of All.* Camarillo, CA: DeVorss & Co, 1997.

Angelou, Maya. *I Know Why The Caged Bird Sings*. New York: Bantam Books, 1971.

Bach, Richard. *Jonathan Livingston Seagull*. New York: Pocket Books, 1973.

Byrne, Rhonda. *The Secret*. New York: Atria Books/Beyond Words, 2006.

Carnegie, Dale. *How To Win Friends And Influence People*. 1936. Reprint. New York: Pocket Books, 1990.

Dyer, Wayne. *You'll See It When You Believe It: The Way To Your Personal Transformation*. New York: Harper Paperbacks, 2001.

Enright, Robert. *www.thepowerofforgiveness.com*

Gardner, Howard. *Frames of Mind: Theory of Multiple Intelligences*. New York: Basic Books, 1983.

Gardner, Howard. *Multiple Intelligences: New Horizons*. New York: Basic Books, 2006.

Giblin, Les. *How To Have Confidence and Power In Dealing With People.* New York: Prentice Hall, 1985.
Hill, Napoleon. *Law Of Success*. Evanston, IL: Success Unlimited, 1977.

Hogan, Kevin. *The Psychology of Persuasion: How To Persuade Others To Your Way Of Thinking*. Gretna, LA: Pelican Publishing, 1996.

Hogan, Kevin. *The Science Of Influence: How To Get Anyone To Say Yes In 8 Minutes Or Less*. Hoboken, NJ: John Wiley and Sons, 2005.

Hogan, Kevin, with Bob Beverley, Dave Lakhani, and Blair Warren. *The Secret Behind The Secret Law Of Attraction*. Eagan, MN: Network 3000 Publishing, 2007.

Holy Bible, King James Version.

Holy Bible, Greek Translation.

Johnson, Mark. *The Body In The Mind: The Bodily Basis Of Meaning, Imagination, And Reason.* Chicago: University of Chicago Press, 1990.

Kirvan, John. *God Hunger: Discovering The Mystic In All Of Us*. Notre Dame, IN: Sorin Books, 1999.

Kirvan, John. *Raw Faith: Nurturing The Believer In All Of Us.* Notre Dame, IN: Sorin Books, 2000.

Kushner, Harold. *When Bad Things Happen To Good People.* New York: Avon Publishing, 1983.

Lakhani, Dave. *Persuasion: The Art Of Getting What Your Want*. Hoboken, NJ: John Wiley and Sons, 2005.

Mandino, Og. *The Greatest Salesman In The World.* New York: Bantam Books, 1983.

McGill, Ormond, and Shelley Stockwell. *The Search For Cosmic Consciousness: The Hypnosis Book Einstein Would Have Loved.* Rancho Palos Verdes, CA: Creativity Unlimited Press, 2000.

Mourkogiannis, Nikos. *Purpose: The Starting Point of Great Companies.* New York: Palgrave Macmillan, 2006.

Ruiz, Don Miguel. *The Four Agreements: A Practical Guide To Personal Freedom A Toltec Wisdom Book.* San Rafael, CA: Amber-Allen Publishing, 1997.

Ryle, Gilbert. *The Concept of Mind.* Chicago: University of Chicago Press, 2000.

Schuller, Robert. *It's Possible.* New York: Fawcett Books, 1981.

Schuller, Robert. *Tough Times Never Last, But Tough People Do.* New York: Bantam, 1984.

Seabury, David. *The Art of Selfishness.* New York: Pocket Books, 1990.

Stockwell, Shelley. *Denial Is Not A River In Egypt: Overcome Addiction, Compulsion And Fear With Dr. Stockwell's Self Hypnosis System.* Rancho Palos Verdes, CA: Creativity Unlimited Press, 2002.

Thomas, Nigel. *www.imagery-imagination.com*

Vitale, Joe, and Jeffrey Gitomer. *There's A Customer Born Every Minute: P.T. Barnum's Amazing 10 "Rings Of Power" For Creating Fame, Fortune, And A Business Empire Today Guaranteed.* Hoboken, NJ: John Wiley and Sons, 2006.

Waitley, Denis. *The Psychology Of Winning.* New York: Berkley, 1984.

Warren, Rick. *Purpose Driven Life.* Grand Rapids, MI: Zondervan, 2007.

Weber, Max. *The Protestant Ethic And The Spirit Of Capitalism.* Rockford, IL: BN Publishing, 2008.

www.abcnews.go.com/GMA/LifeStages/story?id=3167970

www.bls.gov

www.dictionary.com

www.discoverdanjones.co.uk

www.familytabletime.com

www.interbrand.com

www.mayoclinic.org/news2008-mchi/4403.html

www.plato.stanford.edu/entries/friendship/

www.wikipedia.com

Scientific Case Study References

Chapter 3
Association for Psychological Science (2009, September 8). Knowing Me, Myself and I: What Psychology Can Contribute To Self-knowledge. *ScienceDaily*. Retrieved December 20, 2009, from http://wwwsciencedaily.com/releases/2009/07/090716113258.htm

Chapter 4
Rush University Medical Center (2009, June 18). Having A Higher Purpose In Life Reduces Risk Of Death Among Older Adults. *ScienceDaily*. Retrieved December 10, 2009, from http://www.sciencedaily.com/releases/2009/06/090615144207.htm

Chapter 5
Association for Psychological Science (2009, April 15). Power of Imagination Is More Than Just A Metaphor. *ScienceDaily*. Retrieved December 10, 2009, from http://www.sciencedaily.com/2009/04/090414153527.htm

Chapter 6
University of Exeter (2009, March 3). Why Sporting Heroes Should Thank Their Friends. *ScienceDaily*. Retrieved December 20, 2009, from http://www.sciencedaily.com/releases/2009/0903031002616.htm

NOW (Netherlands Organization for Scientific Research)(2009, May 27). Half Of Your Friends Lost In Seven Years, Social Network Study Finds. *ScienceDaily*. Retrieved December 20, 2009, from http://www.sciencedaily.com/releases/2009/0905271 11907.htm

Chapter 7
Kansas State University (2009, August 25). Employees Who Are Engaged In Their Work Have Happier Home Life. *ScienceDaily*. Retrieved January 19, 2010, from http://www.sciencedaily.com/releases/2009/08/0908 24115911.htm

Chapter 8
Springer Science & Business Media (2009, January 12). Spirituality Is Key To Kids' Happiness, Study Suggests. *ScienceDaily*. Retrieved January 7, 2010, from http://www.sciencedaily.com/releases/2009/01/0901 08082904.htm

Character In Action - Toyko
CBS News Sunday Morning. April 18, 2004. Interview conducted by Barry Petersen.

Index

About Ken Owens

Ken Owens is a human-potential consultant in the areas of motivation, sales and personal development. He has over 20 years of corporate and small business management experience. As an Ordained Minister, Ken has worked with many individuals, along with group sessions for numerous non-profit organizations.

Ken is a Certified Stress Management Consultant with the International Association of Counselors and Therapists, Board Certified and Registered Hypnotherapist by both the American Board of Hypnotherapy and the Professional Board of Hypnotherapy in Canada, Certified Sales Trainer and an Instructor with the International Hypnosis Federation.

Ken blends his corporate sales and management experience with his 10 years of crisis counseling and training expertise, along with several degrees in Liberal Arts, Business Management, Counseling and Therapy.

Speaking programs range from one-hour overviews or keynote addresses to full-day in-service programs and weekend workshops. Let Ken help you and your staff take the first step in a positive change toward a happier, healthier and more productive life filled with character!

For booking Ken Owens: www.TheKenOwens.com

Ordering Information

For individual copies of this book:

Check with your local bookstore or with your favorite
online book seller. Also available at
www.Amazon.com

Case-lot orders for resale, educational and non-profit
purposes:

www.PersonalDynamicsPublishing.com

For additional products available from Ken Owens:

www.Store.TheKenOwens.com

Additional free products, services and information for
readers of this book:

www.BrandingYourCharacter.com

Ordering Information

For individual copies of this book:

Check with your local bookstore or with your favorite online book seller. Also available at
www.Amazon.com

Case-lot orders for resale, educational and non-profit purposes:

www.PersonalDynamicsPublishing.com

For additional products available from Ken Owens:

www.Store.TheKenOwens.com

Additional free products, services and information for readers of this book:

www.BrandingYourCharacter.com

Made in the USA
Charleston, SC
27 January 2012